INTRODUCTION

GPVTS has become increasingly more popular over the past few years, with many deaneries seeing the number of applications increasing from a few hundreds to a few thousands over a short period of time. Consequently, the recruitment process has become very competitive and selective.

At the same time, deaneries have been keen to reduce the potential for plagiarism as well as the extent to which candidates obtained help from external sources for the completion of shortlisting questions. To this end, they have taken to inviting candidates to write the answers to their shortlisting questions in an exam style environment, where the candidates' full potential can be fully and unambiguously tested. Whether this move stems from excessive paranoia or from a real need is irrelevant; it has become a reality that each potential GP has to deal with.

The purpose of this book is to provide you with the tools to prepare effectively for these shortlisting questions by helping you think about the attributes that each question is testing and by explaining how you can derive answers that will have a positive impact on your overall shortlisting score.

In this book you will also find a wide range of questions that were asked in previous years by all deaneries, together with explanations about how you can approach and answer each question.

Best of luck!

Olivier Picard
ISCMedical

Interview Skills Consulting

SHORTLISTING

QUESTIONS

FOR

GPVTS

Olivier Picard BSc (Hons) MSc

Interview Skills Consulting

Published by ISCMedical
Suite 434, Hamilton House, Mabledon Place, London WC1H 9BB
Tel: 0845 226 9487

First Published: January 2006
Reprinted February 2006
Reprinted March 2006
Second Edition: April 2006

ISBN 978-1-905812-00-4 (1-905812-00-0)
A catalogue record for this book is available from the British Library.

CONTENTS

ISCMEDICAL
Interview Skills Consulting

An introduction to shortlisting questions

Shortlisting questions are designed to test a range of personal attributes that are essential for a GP. As such, GP recruiters will be interested in hearing about your personal experience of these various skills and attributes, and will require you to demonstrate through your answers that you are a good match for their requirements.

What are the requirements?

Before you can even attempt to answer any shortlisting question, you MUST familiarise yourself with the skills and attributes that you will be expected to demonstrate. These skills and attributes can be found in the person specification for GPs. Essentially they can be summarised as follows:

Attributes / Skills	What it means
Good clinical skills and lateral thinking ability.	You must have a good clinical knowledge and should be able to combine that knowledge to your own judgement to resolve practical issues in a safe and sound manner. You must be able to make sense of all the information you possess. You should also be able to think beyond the obvious and to be open to new ideas to find creative solutions to concrete problems.
Integrity	You must take responsibility for your actions, which includes admitting when you have made mistakes. You must respect others, their skills and contributions. You should also be able to defend your own position and that of your team.

Good Communication Skills	You should be able to communicate equally and openly with colleagues and patients, probing appropriately whenever required.
	You should adapt to the person that you are addressing, using different communication styles and levels depending on the situation.
	You should be sensitive and empathetic towards your patients, make them feel at ease, and demonstrate a genuine interest in their problems.
Organisational & Administration Skills	You are expected to plan, structure and organise your work appropriately. You should also know when and to whom to delegate the work.
	You should have good time management skills and make full use of available IT solutions.
	You should be able to work well and keep calm under pressure. You should be aware of your own limitation, an ability to know when and where to look for help.
	You should also "have a life" outside medicine!
Good Team Work and Managerial Skills	You must work well with others by cooperating and collaborating as necessary to get things done.
	You must be able to negotiate with colleagues and motivate the members of your team. You should contribute to the decision-making process and ensure that you develop good relationships with colleagues, based on trust. You must make efficient use of the resources available to you.

How do shortlisting questions test these skills?

Shortlisting questions typically ask for examples of situations where you demonstrated one or more of the above skills. They encourage you to demonstrate your understanding and application of these skills through practical scenarios. The skills may be tested either at a general level (for example teamwork) or at a more specific level (for example your ability to resolve complex situations by using your initiative).

Questions often explicitly name the skills that are being tested, but in some cases you are left to guess what the questions are driving at, which can make it more difficult to answer. For this reason, you should take a step back before you rush into answering the questions so that you can determine the skills that you want to discuss or demonstrate. This will allow you to plan your answers accordingly.

General points to answer shortlisting questions.

Because the shortlisting process has been continuously evolving over the past few years, it is difficult to generalise in a few sentences what deaneries have been doing until now. As deaneries consolidate their recruitment process, the marking process will evolve further. However there are a number of factors which are important to achieve a high ranking score and you should bear these in mind at all times. These will be addressed throughout the book, but here is a useful summary:

- Make sure you address the depth of the skill that you are demonstrating. Do not just paraphrase the question.

- If you are asked for specific examples, discuss specific situations, not general scenarios to which you are regularly exposed. There is a specific technique to address example questions that we will describe later.

- If you are asked for a list of any sort (for example a list of reasons for wanting to become a GP, or how you keep your knowledge up-to-date, etc), try to identify 5 items that you can discuss. If you can't (or if the number of words is too short for you to achieve this, discuss at least 3 items).

- Be personal. If you are asked about your achievements, explain why they were important to you; if you are asked the reasons for becoming a GP, explain why these reasons matter to you; if you are asked to demonstrate how you handled a particular situation, go into detail about what you did, how you did it and, almost the most important aspect, why you did it.

- Be specific. If the number of words permits it, you should back up your argument with examples that demonstrate that you have a practical understanding of the skill, even if no example was asked for.

- Do not be tempted to address more than what the question is asking for. The form is not a free-for-all debate on your abilities to become a GP but is testing specific skills. The more words you waste, the lower your score will be.

- Do not be tempted to cheat on the number of words. Although recruiters will typically have a tolerance margin of 10%, any more than that will cost you valuable marks. Although no one will count the words one by one, recruiters will have a rough idea of how many lines they should be expecting to see.

- Before you answer any questions at all, read them all. Some questions may complement one another and, if you do not pay attention, you run the risk of repeating yourself. For example, the following three complementary questions were all asked in the same form:
  - ➤ Why do you want to become a GP?
  - ➤ What attributes do you have that will make you a good GP?
  - ➤ How have you strengths and weaknesses influenced your career choices?

- Identify the best format to answer the question. Some questions can easily be answered in a bullet point or list format. For example, to describe why you would make a good GP or to describe how you keep your skills up to date, you can easily have four or five headings that you can develop independently. However, if you are asked to describe one situation in detail, then an essay-type answer is more appropriate. Bear in mind that the format of your answer and the ease with which the recruiters will be reading it are just as important as the content of the answer itself.

QUESTIONS ASKING FOR EXAMPLES

Interview Skills Consulting

HOW TO HANDLE QUESTIONS ASKING FOR EXAMPLES.

Questions asking for examples have always been popular in application forms. This form of questioning, called "behavioural", stems from the fact that your recruiters are likely to learn a lot more about you by getting you to talk about your past experience than by asking you how you might behave in hypothetical situations. Typical questions are likely to be of the form:

Describe a situation where you played an important role in a team, where you used your communication skills to improve the care of the patient, where you made a mistake, where you failed to communicate effectively, where you were involved in cost savings, etc.

The rules
Although most candidates find such questions difficult, they are in fact relatively easy once you have identified a good example to discuss, provided you follow a number of important rules, as follows.

Rule 1: Make sure you choose a specific example
Many candidates prefer to address vague situations or to speak about their experience in general. For example "Describe a situation where you played an important role in a team" often leads answers of the type "I work in teams all the time, working with colleagues, nurses, etc". Giving such an answer would be missing totally the point of the question. If you read the question correctly it is asking for <u>a situation,</u> i.e. a specific case or project that you handled.

Rule 2: Keep a broad mind
Unless the question specifically calls for it, you do not have to stick to clinical scenarios. There are skills that are sometimes best demonstrated by discussing non-medical situations (for example managerial skills when organising an event). Although it is true that you should as much as possible find examples that are closely related to the context in which you will be working, it is by no means compulsory, especially if your medical examples

6

are not very impressive but you have instead an impressive record outside medicine. In addition, some questions make it clear that you can talk about non-medical situations. Do not hesitate.

Rule 3: Minimise the clinical aspect of the situation that you are describing.

All shortlisting questions are designed to test your generic skills, not your clinical skills (these would be assessed through the MCQs/EMQs part of the recruitment process or other types of assessment that deaneries may see fit). Besides, if the recruiters wanted to test your clinical skills in a particular area, they would ask specific clinical questions and would not take the chance that you may or may not address a subject of interest. Instead, look carefully at the question and ask yourself what skills are being tested.

Rule 4: Take some time to identify all the skills you need to demonstrate.

In a question such as "Describe a situation where your communication skills had a positive effect on the management of a patient", it is obvious that the question is testing your ability to communicate (which would include listening, empathy and addressing the needs of the patient). In other more complex questions, such as "Give an example of a situation where you had to deal with a complex situation", there are many skills that you can demonstrate such as:

- Your ability to take initiative as well as work within your own limits.
- Your ability to identify the resources you need to resolve this problem.
- Your ability to seek help from seniors whenever required.
- Your ability to work with your team to achieve the best possible result.
- Your ability to communicate with all parties involved (patients, team, etc.)
- Your ability to document important information.

Taking 30 seconds or so to think about the question and what it is aiming at will help you plan your answer better and will enable you to produce an answer that has a clear focus and sense of direction. If you have only 20 minutes to produce an answer that will make a strong impact, you cannot afford to make a false start and change direction half-way through. Spending a few seconds planning your answer before you start writing will help you enormously.

Rule 5: Ensure that your example is fully relevant and addresses as many of the required skills identified as possible.

Many candidates are so happy to have found one example that they rush into their explanation without thinking whether they are maximising their chances by using it. A bad example will be difficult to explain in detail and will leave a bad impression on the recruiters. For example, discussing your role in the crash team as an example of good team playing will not take you very far. As a member of the crash team, you will only be obeying the orders of the team leader but you will not really be consciously demonstrating the team playing abilities that would be required of a GP (such as taking on board others' ideas, offering support, creating an atmosphere of trust, etc). Choosing a good example is essential (and makes your life easier too!).

Rule 6: Do not be tempted to make things up.

It does not require much training to recognise a liar. Recruiters will be able to spot fairly easily whether you are making things up (unless you are really good at it) simply by the lack of detail that you are providing and the vagueness of your answers. In addition, even if you manage to get through unnoticed, you will not escape a well targeted question at your subsequent interview, where interviewers will ask you for further details on the example set out in your answer. There is only one answer to this: you must prepare good examples before sitting the shortlisting questions session.

Rule 7: Be personal

Use the space you have to describe what YOU did, not what everyone else did (unless it is absolutely relevant to the situation). Too many candidates waste their word allowance discussing what the team did and how the team worked, giving little information about what they themselves did. You must always remember that the point of the recruitment process is to find out about YOU, not about anyone else. Concentrate on the "I" rather than the "We" and don't be afraid of going into a certain amount of detail, provided it is relevant.

Rule 8: Follow the "STAR" technique

The STAR technique, described in the following chapter, provides an easy way to give a focussed and organised answer. Spend some time to apply it to as many examples as you can so that it becomes second nature.

Interview Skills Consulting

THE "STAR" TECHNIQUE

The acronym "**STAR**" stands for Situation Task Action Result. It is a universally recognised communication technique designed to enable you to provide a meaningful and complete answer to questions asking for examples. At the same time it has the advantage of being simple enough to be applied easily.

Many recruiters and interviewers will have been trained in using this structure. Even if they have not, they will recognise its value when they see it. The information will be given to them in a structure manner and as a result they will become more receptive to the messages you are trying to communicate.

Step 1 – Situation or Task

Describe the situation that you were confronted to or the task that needed to be accomplished. This section is merely setting the context for the "Action" section so that the recruiters can understand the story from start to finish. You should therefore aim to make is concise and informative, concentrating solely on what is useful to the story and the message that you are trying to communicate in your answer.

For example if the question is asking you to describe a situation where you had to deal with a difficult person, explain how you came to meet that person and why they were being difficult. If the question is asking for an example of team work, explain the task that you had to undertake as a team.

Step 2 – Action

This is the most important section as it is where you will need to demonstrate and highlight the skills and personal attributes that the question is testing. Now that you have set the context of your story, you need to explain what you did. In doing so, you will need to remember the following:

▪ Be personal i.e. talk about you, not the rest of the team.
▪ Go into some detail. Do not assume that they will guess what you mean.
▪ Steer clear of clinical information, unless it is crucial to your story.
▪ Highlight all your actions that demonstrate that you have the right skills.
▪ Explain what you did, how you did it, and why you did it.

9

WHAT YOU DID & HOW YOU DID IT.

Obviously the recruiters will want to know how you reacted to the situation. This is where you can start selling some important skills. For example, you may want to describe how you used the team to achieve a particular objective and how you used your communication skills to keep everyone updated on progress, etc.

WHY YOU DID IT

This is probably the most crucial part of your answer. Recruiters want to know that you are using a variety of generic skills in order to achieve your objectives. Therefore you must be able to demonstrate in your answer that you are taking actions because you understand their purpose and what they will achieve, not simply because you got lucky.

For example, when dealing with breaking bad news, it would be easy to say: "I took the patient to a separate room and discussed the test results." However it would not give a good idea of what drove you to act in this manner and would look like a fairly standard answer. Why did you take the patient to a separate room?

By highlighting the reasons behind your reaction as follows, you would make a greater impact: "In order to create a comfortable environment for the patient, I took him to a separate room and asked the secretary to ensure that we were not disturbed." This shows your attention to the needs of the patient, and your use of the team to achieve this. These are two of the skills that they would be looking for.

Step 3 – Result

Explain what happened eventually, how it all ended. Also use the opportunity to describe what you accomplished and what you learnt in that situation. This helps you make the answer personal and enables you to highlight further skills.

Often the question will ask explicitly for all these elements by asking you for example to describe how you would have done things differently. If it does not, then you must try to include as many of these elements as possible without being prompted. This will help the recruiters determine the extent to which you are able to think laterally and completely about a particular issue.

COMMUNICATION

TEAM PLAYING

LEADERSHIP

COMMUNICATION SKILLS

There are a number of areas of communication in which a doctor must excel. They would generally fall under one of the following two categories:

1 - Active Listening Skills

This is closely linked with empathy, which all doctors are required to demonstrate. Empathy is characterised by a personal ability to see a situation from the other person's point of view and relates to the following behaviours:

- Being attentive and acknowledging – this is usually achieved through simple body language such as an open posture and good eye contact. It also includes nodding at the appropriate time etc.

- Reflecting the other person's feelings and experiences.

- Probing in a supportive manner.

- Providing feedback, being supportive, showing warmth and being caring.

- Checking with the other person whether your interpretation of a situation is accurate.

- Knowing when to stay quiet and simply give the other person the time they need.

This applies equally to your dealings with patients and colleagues. The impact of good active listening skills is a better relationship, an ability to build a rapport and generate mutual trust, which is crucial in your dealings with everyone. This results in better care for patients and a better working relationship with your colleagues.

2 – Conveying messages in a clear and effective manner

The skill involved in conveying messages clearly and effectively resides principally in your ability to adapt your communication to your audience. This includes:

- Using clear and unambiguous language.

- Checking the understanding of your audience and adapting your message to it.

- Having a clear idea of what you are trying to communicate.

- Taking account of prior knowledge and personal circumstances of your audience.

- Using the appropriate level of jargon.

- Choosing the most appropriate medium to communicate (written / face-to-face / email / telephone / diagrams / posters / models, etc).

This applies equally whether you are giving instructions to a junior colleague, presenting issues to a senior colleague, teaching others, giving a presentation to a peer group, breaking bad news, writing notes, handing over, or discussing issues with patients.

ISCMEDICAL
Interview Skills Consulting

TEAM PLAYING

Team playing is often confused with leadership. One of the reasons for this confusion is the fact that as a colleague, you cannot be categorised simply as a "player", a "leader" or even a "manager". You are often all of these at different times of the day. Attend a multi-disciplinary team meeting and you are simply one representative amongst five or six others. Your equal status makes you a team member. Direct a ward round or give instructions to a group of nurses and you become a leader.

Attributes of a good team player

- **Understands his role in the team and how it fits within the whole picture.**
  In order to get on within a team, team players must have a thorough understanding of what they need to achieve and what is expected of them. They must also understand what is expected of others so that they can work with them effectively.

- **Treats others with respect. Is supportive.**
  Team players treat fellow team members with courtesy and consideration. They show understanding and provide the appropriate support to other team members to help get the job done. Effective team players deal with other people in a professional manner.

- **Is willing to help.**
  Good team players go beyond any differences they may have with other team members and find ways to work together to get work done. They respond to requests for assistance and take the initiative to offer help.

- **Is flexible and adaptable.**
  Good team players adapt to ever-changing situations without complaining or resisting. Flexible team members can consider different points of views and compromise when needed. They do not hold rigidly to a point of view especially when the team needs to move forward to make a decision or get something done. They must strike a compromise between holding on to their own beliefs and convictions whilst respecting and taking on board other colleagues' opinions.

- **Communicates constructively and listens actively.**
  Teams need people who speak up and express their thoughts and ideas clearly, directly, honestly, and with respect for others and for the work of the team. Good listeners are essential for teams to function effectively. Teams need team players who can absorb, understand, and consider ideas and points of view from other people without debating and arguing every point. Such a team member also can receive criticism without reacting defensively. Finally, a good team member shares information with colleagues and keeps them up to date about progress on his or her assignments.

- **Is reliable. Takes responsibility and ownership of his role.**
  A good team member should do everything possible to deliver on his assignments on time and with the level of quality expected from him by the rest of the team. He should get things done and do their fair share to work hard and meet commitments. You can count on them to deliver good performance all the time, not just some of the time. He should also be relied upon to admit their mistakes and proactively sorting them out.

ISCMEDICAL
Interview Skills Consulting

LEADERSHIP

Attributes of a good leader

- **Has clear objectives and communicates them effectively to the team.**
  In order to lead a team, a leader must have a clear sense of direction, and clear objectives. (This is often referred to by candidates as "a vision", although this term is very business-like and really only applies to the higher management echelons). A good leader is able to communicate those objectives clearly to the rest of the team so that they can take responsibility to achieve their own goals.

- **Leads by example.**
  A good leader is effective only if he is being followed by his team. He must engender respect from his colleagues by showing a good example. A leader needs to be enthusiastic, competent and confident. He needs to demonstrate that he works at least as hard as he expects others to do.

- **Understands and motivates his team.**
  A good leader must understand the strengths, weaknesses and aspirations of each team member. This enables him to share responsibilities accordingly. He motivates his team towards achievement by:

  - ➤ Praising and encouraging others;
  - ➤ Rewarding colleagues (This could be through financial incentives, promotion, or by involving team members in specific projects);
  - ➤ Empowering people & giving them responsibilities and freedom;
  - ➤ Making himself available.

- **Communicates and interacts well with his team.**
A good leader should listen to the input and ideas of the team and should take them on board when making decisions. Communicating constantly with the team is also important for the leader, in order to have a good idea of how the team functions, of grievances or any other problems which makes it easier to anticipate and resolve conflict.

- **Recognises the need for change and implements it. Is a decision maker.**
A good leader is not static and constantly seeks new ways of working and improving. A good leader is able to take on board all the input he receives and to make a decision on that basis. He does not seek short-term popularity at the expense of achievement.

- **Is flexible**
A good leader will adapt his leadership style to the demands of particular situations and the individuals involved. Some situations or individuals will require him to take a hands-on approach whilst other may require him to take a step back and be more hands off.

ANALYSIS OF PAST SHORTLISTING QUESTIONS

Interview Skills Consulting

HEALTH WARNING

In order to assist you in writing successful answers to your shortlisting questions, we have gathered a long list of questions asked over the past few years during the shortlisting process.

These questions cover a broad range of skills and areas. For each of them, we have described the immediate reaction that the question may generate, as well as tips about how to approach the questions to find a suitable content.

For some of these questions we have tried to provide model answers that will give you an idea about the type of content, structure and style required. In many cases, it would have proven unnecessary or repetitive to do so and we have instead provided information that should help you derive your own answer.

IMPORTANT NOTE
Although you may inspire yourself from the examples given, you are advised to prepare answers of your own that draw upon your experience and make you stand out from the crowd. Indeed it would be unwise to risk having the same answer as hundreds of other candidates! Don't be afraid to be yourself. We all prefer an individual GP with a personality rather than a clone…

ISCMEDICAL
Interview Skills Consulting

QUESTION 1

Team working is essential in General Practice. Give an example of a recent situation you have participated in where teamwork was important. What role did you play? What did you learn from this experience?

First impression

This question is very explicit. The introduction tells you that they are testing your team working abilities. In addition, it is a question asking for an example and they are guiding you through the STAR technique:

Situation/Task: Give an example of …
Action: What role did you play?
Result: What did you learn from this experience?

Please also take note of the request for a RECENT situation. This usually means in the past 6 to 12 months.

How to approach the question?

1 - Recall the attributes of a good team player (since you will need to demonstrate them throughout your answer). From a practical point of view, essentially you want to present the image of someone who:

- Has a good relationship with colleagues and is able to work with them to get the work done. Is willing to take on his/her share of the workload, and to offer his help and support to others.

- Keeps communication going within the team by keeping his/her colleagues informed about what they are doing and shares any other information that may be relevant.

- Takes the initiative to resolve issues and discuss problems with the team. This could include negotiating with colleagues if necessary.

- Ensures that he/she carries out his/her work properly and seeks help if they are encountering a problem.

2 – Identify a situation in your recent past where you have had the opportunity to demonstrate these skills, making sure that the example you choose enables you to demonstrate as many team playing skills as possible. This could be a situation where you:

- Participated in the organisation of an event or project such as organising a seminar, regular teaching sessions, health camps, awareness programmes, etc.

- Had to deal with a complex patient, where team playing was important. In order to make the answer interesting you would need to find an example where you had to deal with a multi-disciplinary team for example. You could then explain how you participated to the debate about the management and ongoing care of the patient, and how you interacted with all members of the team to achieve a safe discharge.

- Had to deal with an emergency by using the resources available on the nurses' and junior doctors' side, whilst maintaining constant communication with your seniors at all times so that they could have an input into the process and would be fully briefed by the time they arrived. Note that in order to highlight as many skills as possible, you would need to ensure that the situation is complex enough to show how important YOUR role was too. For examples, if your seniors are there with you and they are managing the situation themselves (e.g. crash call), you are losing the opportunity to emphasise the communication aspect of your role in keeping them up-to-date.

Example of ineffective answers

Example 1

"I work every day as part of a team, dealing with colleagues, nurses and other doctors. I am aware of my limitations and seek help when necessary, and I communicate well with everyone in the team. I am willing to help and motivate others."

This answer is too vague and general. In fact, it does little more than summarising the job description. Also, it does not actually answer the question, which is asking for an example of a recent situation i.e. a specific scenario in which you were involved.

Example 2

"I had an elderly patient who wanted to self-discharge because she was worried about her dog. I talked to the nurse and the consultant, and eventually the patient agreed to stay one more day. The patient left the hospital the next day and was happy with the way she had been handled."

This answer starts well by explaining the context which will lead to a team action to be started. The main problem is that the "Action" section contains very little information. There are plenty of other aspects that can be exploited.

- Why did you talk to the nurse or the consultant? Most likely because the consultant is responsible for the patient and had to be informed. As for the nurse, it might have been because she had a good relationship with the patient and a good understanding of their psychological issues too through the rapport she had built with that patient. This needs to be explained.

- Did you do anything else that would have made you a good team player? Like taking the initiative to contact social services or ask the patient if the relatives could be involved? (They can become part of the team too).

This answer basically needs more detail about what was done and why it was done.

Finally, the "Result" section is partially addressing the wrong point. As well as highlighting that the problem was satisfactorily resolved, it should emphasise that this was the result of team work.

Example of an effective answer

Three months ago, I was on-call taking admissions from GPs and A&E. I was the only SHO on-site, with my Registrar being busy in theatre and my consultant being on-call from home.

A patient presented with <Emergency> which required admission to theatre. Whilst I was stabilising the patient, I asked the house officer to call the Registrar in theatre as it is protocol to inform my seniors for all such cases. The Registrar informed him that he would be busy for at least two hours and I therefore took the decision to call the consultant as well, who announced that he would come in as soon as he could.

At the same time I asked one of the nurse practitioners to call the anaesthetist and help prepare the theatre so that everything would be ready by the time the consultant arrived. Throughout this time I kept in constant communication with the consultant in order to ensure that he was fully briefed.

The patient was taken to theatre within minutes of the consultant's arrival and made a successful recovery. By coordinating the team at a time that was stressful for all involved (patient and doctors) I helped achieve this result. This taught me how crucial communication is in ensuring that the whole team functions well.

Note the absence of much detailed clinical information (totally irrelevant for the purpose of highlighting team playing), the concise but informative introduction, and the manner in which the main components of team playing are highlighted throughout the example, including:

- Recognising protocol, and your limitations.

- Informing your seniors and keeping them up to date about developments.

- Informing other colleagues about developments that are relevant to them (the anaesthetist).

- Using other team members to help out, based on their skills level.

- Getting things done (stabilising the patient, preparing the theatre, etc.)

Also note how the conclusion keeps the mind of the reader focused on your skills by not only explaining the outcome in a concise manner but also highlighting what you did that made it possible to achieve it, and what you learnt from it.

Final comments

This scenario could be adapted with very little work to cover other types of example. For example, it is a good example of a situation where you used your initiative or a situation where you had to work under stress (although you would need to place a slightly different emphasis on each aspect of the answer to achieve the desired impact).

Identifying examples that are complex enough to cover several skills is a good trick to minimise your preparation (although you should ensure that you use different examples for each question in the exam).

QUESTION 2

Describe a situation when you needed to demonstrate empathy towards a patient. What did you do well and what could you have done better?

First Impression

No real surprise about what skill is being tested. The question is very explicit. Here again the question asks for an example, so you need to identify a fairly recent but specific patient that you dealt with. Also bear in mind the second half of the question (often forgotten). There is no harm is being open about how you could have handled the situation better since communication (and building a rapport through empathy) is a process that you are constantly learning to perfect.

How to approach the question?

1 - Think about what empathy is about.

Essentially this is about being attentive and acknowledging the patient's needs, probing in a supportive manner, providing feedback, being supportive, showing warmth and being caring (See section on Communication)

2 – Identify a suitable situation.

Empathy is a notoriously difficult skill to talk about and to demonstrate because it deals with feelings that are not always easy to translate on paper. To maximise your chances, you should aim to identify a patient who was in a particularly difficult or vulnerable position. This may be easier for those who have done medicine rather than surgery. The types of situations you may wish to discuss include situations where you:

- Had to break bad news.
- Had to deal with a patient who was worried about a chronic disease.
- Dealt with someone who was frightened (patient before an operation, elderly person who did not want to be discharged, etc)

- Dealt with someone who was assaulted, abused, wounded, etc
- Dealt with a recently bereaved relative (miscarriage, etc)
- Dealt with people with sensitive problems (infertility, etc)
- Dealt with people in difficult situations (no fixed address, recently unemployed, divorce, asylum seeker, etc)

Examples of ineffective answers

Example 1
"In my job as an SHO in Oncology, I often have to break bad news. I approach them sensitively and make sure that I take them to a separate room where we cannot be disturbed, I explain to the patient the tests that we have done and make sure that I check their understanding ..."

This answer is ineffective for two reasons:

- It does not deal with a specific example and is too vague.

- The answer briefly mentions empathy/sensitivity at the start but then quickly deviates into a different question: "How do you break bad news?" This is not what the question is calling for.

Example 2
"As an SHO in Oncology I had to break the news to one of my patients that she had carcinoma of the colon. I approached her sensitively and empathically, making sure that she was fine, and answering all her questions..."

This answer is on the right tract but almost tries to cram too much information at the same time. Rather than just stating that you were sensitive and empathic, you should put it into the specific context of this patient. You can see how the above text can almost be used as such for any example – this tends to indicate that a more personal approach is needed.

Example of an effective answer

Whilst working in A&E I saw a young Asian woman who was 6 months pregnant. She was very timid but even so appeared to be quite distressed.

Seeing that she was alone and vulnerable, I thought about how I would feel if I were in her situation and about how I would want to be treated. I took her to a cubicle away from most of the bustle of the department. I took my time, did not rush her and started to take a history. She became a little tearful and so I spoke in a softer tone. However I knew by her composure that she wanted to tell me more so I gently asked about why she was so upset. Suddenly she just let out all her emotions. She explained that she had miscarried twice before and that her husband and his family thought she was an unfit wife. I could tell she was relieved to confide in someone. Her medical complaint turned out to be minor and with the good rapport we had built she trusted the diagnosis.

Overall I found that actively listening, preparing the scene and mirroring her pace was useful. Using words that were non-threatening and from her own vocabulary also helped. In hindsight I felt that I could have given her more space to talk and I would also involve another person such as a staff nurse who could also reassure the patient.

Final comments

There are few other ways in which your empathy/listening skills may be tested. Other questions include:

- Describe a time when your understanding and empathy towards a patient contributed positively to their health.

- Tell me about a time where your communication skills made a difference to the standard of care being provided to a patient.

Essentially, these call for a similar type of answer, though you should make sure you fully address the question and, in this case, that you explicitly emphasise how your behaviour impacted on the patient.

QUESTION 3

Describe a time when you were unsure whether what you were being told represented the patient's true thoughts or feelings. How did you recognise this? What did you do about it?

First Impression

This question seems more complex that the others since it does not explicitly request information about a given skill. Also the type of example that the question is asking for can be quite tricky to find if you haven't got much experience.

How to approach the question?

1 – Think about a type of situation where this might happen.
The question does not tell you whether it is the patient who is not telling you his true thoughts, or whether it is a relative who is telling you something that is not in agreement with the patient's thoughts or feelings.

If it is the patient, then it may be because they are frightened of what will happen to them if they revealed their thoughts or feelings. This may be a patient who is scared about their own health problems, a patient who hides part of their history to avoid confronting the reality of their illness, or an elderly patient who is keen to have their health problems resolved but is not keen to be taken into care, or is worried about becoming a burden on their relatives.

If it is a relative, it may be that they are trying to forcibly influence the patient into a position that suits them rather than the patient.

Having thought about the question in a general manner, you should now be equipped to find a real-life example in your own experience.

2– Identify the skills that you want to demonstrate in this example.
The question is asking you how you recognised that there was an issue and what you did about it. Recognising the issue will come from your own judgement of the situation based maybe on inconsistencies in the story that you are getting from the patient, their body language, the way which they express themselves (for example by being vague), etc. Ultimately this will come from your ability to listen to the patient and probe accordingly – in essence, your communication skills. This is the easy bit!

Dealing with the issue is more complex and essentially requires you to gain the patient's confidence in order to put them back on the right track. This may involve:

- Communication (empathy, listening skills in order to build trust); there is a reason behind this situation and you must identify it quickly. This requires a lot of diplomacy and sensitivity.

- Team work. You may need to involve:

  ➢ a nurse – they often have a more in-depth relationship with the patient simply by the fact they may be more empathic than doctors and have more time to spend with patients.

  ➢ the GP – if there is time to make decisions and the patient can be helped through counseling or simply by having an opportunity to discuss issues.

  ➢ the relatives, if needed. They may be crucial in reassuring the patient.

  ➢ your seniors (identify your limitations!)

In addition, if the relatives are causing the problem (for example by forcing the patient to adopt a particular attitude against his/her will) you may have to use other tools to minimise their possible negative influence on the patient. This could include involving seniors, showing an assertive but sensitive behaviour, spending time with the relatives (after all there may be a valid reason or fear behind their behaviour), etc.

Because this is likely to be an unusual situation, you will need to demonstrate your initiative and lateral thinking to come up with a creative and effective solution.

Example of an ineffective answer

"One of my patients wanted to self-discharge because she felt her dog would be in danger if she did not get back home as soon as possible. I suggested that she called a relative so that they could look after the animal but she was adamant that she needed to do it herself.

This prompted me to think that there was more to her story and, after much discussion, I concluded that she was worried about the anaesthesia. In order to resolve the situation I arranged for the patient to have a second discussion with the anaesthetist and also arranged for a nurse to sit in with her. After the discussion the patient was happy and went through with the operation."

This answer is not "bad". It has a number of positive aspects:
- It deals with a specific situation.
- The introduction is fairly descriptive and effective in setting out the situation.
- It addresses the right type of issue.

On the negative side, it describes what the doctor did, but not really why he thought or acted like this. In other words, the answer needs more depth and needs to highlight how the doctor used his skills to resolve the situation.

What can be improved?
Look at the following statement: "*This prompted me to think that there was more to her story and, after much discussion, I concluded that she was worried about the anaesthesia*".

Essentially, it looks as if the doctor has jumped to a conclusion without really explaining how it came about. The whole process has been summarised by "after much discussion". Since the question is asking how you recognised that there was an issue to be addressed, you would need to go into more detail about that conversation and discuss how you spent time with the patient, discussing the situation and their fears, eventually picking up on parts of the

conversation that seemed to indicate that she was in fear of anaesthesia. At the same time you would need to emphasise how you used your listening skills and empathy to gain the patient's trust and confidence.

Maybe you asked a nurse to have a conversation with the patient instead because you felt she had a good relationship with the patient and that the patient would open up more easily to someone of the same sex. Either way, it does not matter provided you explain how your actions justified your trail of thoughts and provided you address the skills that you used.

Example of an effective answer

"One of my patients wanted to self-discharge because she felt that her dog would be in danger if she did not get back home as soon as possible. I suggested that she called a relative so that they could look after the animal but she was adamant that she needed to do it herself. This prompted me to think that there was more to her story and that maybe she feared the operation she was due to have the next day.

During a quiet period, I asked a nurse to make sure that I would not be disturbed. I sat down with the patient and asked her gently to tell me about her dog. I listened patiently to her, showing an interest in her story and occasionally asking questions. As the patient opened up to me, I felt more comfortable introducing the subject of her own health and the operation. I could feel that she wanted to express her fears but that she was reluctant to admit to the problem, perhaps because she did not want to appear foolish. I gently explained what the operation entailed and reassured her about the anaesthesia. In order to avoid giving the patient the impression that I was pressurising her, I asked the nurse to spend some time with her. To reassure the patient further, I arranged a meeting with the anaesthetist and arranged for the relatives to discuss the care of the dogs with the patient.

After a few hours of concerted team work and sensitive communication, the patient agreed to remain in hospital and the surgery went ahead as scheduled, with a successful outcome."

Note how the example above combines team work and communication skills in a relatively detailed manner.

Final comments

To have an impact, you must make sure that your answers are as personal as they can be by drawing into the relevant detail of the experience that you have accumulated over the years.

It is worth spending time carefully choosing a good example as the detail will flow naturally. If you choose an example that is not appropriate or if you are not addressing the skills explicitly within your answer, you will quickly run out of steam and end up producing vague sentences (if you haven't run out of words before then).

The above example also shows you how you can transform an "okay" answer into a much more precise answer simply by expanding on one or two ideas that you raised, highlighting how you used your skills in practice to achieve the desired result.

QUESTION 4

Outline a time when a new and different approach to a patient of yours proved beneficial. What did you do and what was the outcome?

First Impression

The question asks for a different approach. At first glance this could mean either a different way of managing a patient, for example by trying a different type of treatment, or a different way of approaching the patient from a communication point of view.

Bearing in mind that shortlisting questions are not designed to assess your clinical knowledge but your personal skills, you should ensure that you do not fall into the trap of discussing a clinical scenario as it would yield no marks.

How to approach the question?

1 – Identify the type of situation that the question is targeting & then choose a suitable example from your experience.

Essentially the question is asking you to describe a situation where your first approach was unsuccessful and where you then changed your strategy of approach to achieve your objective. This could include situations where:

- a patient was reluctant to go ahead with one of your recommendations and where you had to take a different approach in your communication to make them get the message.

- a patient with whom you used a first approach that revealed some underlying issues, which then prompted you to choose a different approach. For example, you may have adopted a "standard" approach to the problem but then gained information from the patient or otherwise that there were deeper psychological issues at stake, that needed to be resolved as part of the same process.

2 – Identify the skills that you will demonstrate through the scenario.

This question is essentially about testing three skills:

- Your ability to think laterally about a difficult situation, using your knowledge of the patient/the situation and the resources available to you in order to find a solution that will drive you towards a successful outcome. (Note that this could include involving other people such as relatives, other doctors, etc. in which case you may be able to include an element of teamwork in your answer).

- Your communication skills in relation to the patient

- The manner in which you are able to build and maintain a rapport with the patient to achieve your desired objective, whilst not compromising your integrity and preserving respect for the patients' values and choices.

Example of an ineffective answer

> "An obese 42-year old HGV driver came to my clinic with a high blood sugar level. His GP had referred him to the diabetic clinic twice (he had Type 2 diabetes) and, each time, the patient had failed to attend.
>
> Despite my best efforts to explain the situation to the patient and encourage him to attend, he was not listening attentively and was being uncooperative. I felt a stronger approach would be required to kick the patient into action. I told him that unless he was admitted into hospital and treated, there would be long-term complications to his diabetes, such as loss of eyesight, nerve damage, heart disease and stroke. "

The above answer has a lot of good points:
- It deals with a specific example.
- The situation is fairly clear
- The clinical information is reduced to the bare minimum.

What can be improved?

The answer seems a little harsh. Effectively the writer is saying "He wouldn't listen so I scared him to make him comply". This needs to be softened. In particular the writer should spend more time demonstrating how he approached the patient in the first place, with empathy and sensitivity etc to demonstrate why the second approach was necessary.

Also the writer has missed out the "Result" part of the answer. This makes it look very odd and even scary to a point. You simply don't feel that there was a rapport between the patient and the doctor, or any attempt by the doctor to try his very best before escalating his approach. The answer should therefore focus more around the communication aspect and how the doctor interacted with the patient, rather than just about what the doctor felt and what he said.

Example of an effective answer

"An obese 42-year old HGV driver came to my clinic with a high blood sugar level and a urinary tract infection. His history revealed that his GP had referred him to the diabetic clinic twice for Type 2 diabetes and that the patient had failed to attend both appointments. On enquiring about the reasons for his non-attendance, the patient mentioned that he was scared of being prescribed insulin as it would lead to the loss his HGV licence.

My first approach to the patient's reaction was to listen carefully to his words, explaining that I understood his dilemma, but also emphasising the solutions we could find. I took him through the features of Type 2 diabetes and explained that there were ways in which it could be controlled. In view of his worries, I reassured him that insulin would probably not be an option. I felt that the patient was not listening attentively and was being uncooperative. As he had already missed two appointments and was showing few signs of encouragement, I felt that a stronger approach would be required to encourage him to take appropriate action. After discussing the issue with my consultant, I explained to the patient that, unless he was admitted into hospital and treated, there would be long-term complications to his diabetes, such as loss of eyesight, nerve damage, heart disease and stroke.

This resulted in a drastic change in the patient's attitude who very quickly agreed to being admitted. A few months later, the patient thanked me for my empathic but assertive approach as he felt I had saved his life.

ISCMEDICAL
Interview Skills Consulting

This answer is more balanced, showing empathy, discussing with the consultant and then adapting the style of communication to the situation and the patient's reaction.

Final Comments

Without doing some preliminary ground work, it would be easy to mishandle the question by taking a clinical perspective that would lead you straight to disaster. By doing some preliminary thinking before you launch into an answer, you will quickly identify the skills that you can demonstrate. In turn, this will save you a great deal of time when you are actually writing the answer as you will know exactly what you are trying to say.

There is no harm in presenting clinical information as was done above, but only to the extent that it helps towards the story. In the example above, it was necessary to include some in order to demonstrate the gravity of the patient's condition and the extent to which the patient was "scared" into compliance.

Finally, beware of words that may sound harsher than you mean them to be. For example "I told" is very directive whilst "I explained" is softer.

QUESTION 5

Give an example of how you organise your workload. What do you do and what do you use to support this?

First Impression

The question seems fairly straight forward. They also guide you through it by asking what you use to support this. The main problem people have with this question is either that they have no idea about what to say or they know what to say but are not sure about how to put it across in an interesting manner. One issue with such standard question is that there is a risk everyone ends up having the same answer.

Please note that unlike other example questions, this one is asking for a general situation. Otherwise they would be asking for an example where you organised your workload, what did you do etc. This means that you can answer the question more loosely but you still need to be quite specific about what you do. You also need to explain what you do by explaining how it helps you concretely throughout your working day.

How to approach the question?

There is little to guess about this question. Essentially you need to think about your day to day experience and how you make sure you do everything you need to do.

1 - How do you organise your workload?

This will include:

- Making lists of patients and a list of tasks, whether patient related or not. Prioritising your tasks.

- Identifying whether you might require assistance from other people and ensuring they are briefed early enough (and available!)

- Reviewing your list on a regular basis, updating patient details and reprioritising if necessary.

- Delegating tasks to the appropriate colleague / Sharing the workload.

- Working efficiently by initiating the investigations you need to do as early as possible in order to ensure that the results are back on time for when you need them.

- Ensuring that you have the capacity to handle emergencies, firstly by building up some slack into your schedule if you can so that, should something happen, you have time to catch up on the delay that occurred; secondly by identifying who is available for help if needed.

- Making sure that you plan your work in advance as much as you can, for example by reserving slots for specific matters (paperwork, teaching sessions, important meetings) as these may impose constraints onto your schedule. Arranging for cross-cover when needed.

2 – What do you use to support this?

This part of the question related to tools that you might find handy to help you organise your workload. This would include:

- PDA if you have one

- Excel spreadsheet (useful for lists and easy update of information)

- Outlook Calendar or other electronic calendar system

- Secretary – this allows you to sell your team playing abilities!

How to phrase your answer?

The key here is to avoid simply listing the items above as it is a fairly safe bet that most candidates will come up with most of them. Therefore there will be nothing to distinguish you from other people and your answer will not feel personal. To be personal you should try to relate each point you are making to your past experience. For example, instead of saying "I do a list of patients

and prioritise them. I delegate tasks to nurses and PRHOs etc.", you can make a more developed and personal answer by saying something along the following lines:

> "Before the ward round I prepare a list of all patients containing their basic details, diagnosis and summary management plan. After the ward round I have a short discussion with my juniors to agree how we can share the work and prioritise my own workload in relation to their degree of urgency. I make sure that I request all blood tests and book diagnostic tests straight after the ward round so that the results can come back as early as possible. I update my job list throughout the day to take account of developments.
>
> During my job as SHO in Elderly Care, I had to prepare a lot of paperwork for discharge plans and found it useful to allocate a specific slot every day to carry out all administrative tasks, usually before the ward round as I was least likely to be disturbed." Etc.

You can discuss the tools that you use either as a separate section in your answer or by mixing the information with your examples. Whenever you mention a tool, try to explain not just that it is useful but also why it is useful.
For example: "I regularly use a PDA" is informative but if many people say that then there is little information to distinguish between all of you. You could complement this statement by adding something like:

> "As well as helping me keep the information in one place, it enables me to have rapid access to all essential information without having to carry pieces of paper in my pocket. It also helps me being more efficient by giving me access to other forms of electronic information such as drug dosages.

Final Comments
This is one of the easier types of questions as the answer is usually very factual and you do not have to convey complex emotions in words. Generally speaking, for factual questions, you will need to come up with at least five different relevant ideas or issues in order to optimise your marks.

However the difficulty is in making the answer powerful by taking a practical angle, drawing examples from your experience.

Other questions that relate to the same theme include:

- Describe a time when you had a particularly bad day at work due to workload pressures. What strategies did you use to cope both during and after that time? What was the effect? (This one calls for a specific example!)

- People organise their time in different ways. What approaches and strategies do you use to plan and protect your time for training as a doctor? - This is a similar question but with the added element of protecting your training time. Essentially, this is about organising your workload as above to make sure that you are efficient but also about planning set times for training and working with your colleagues to ensure that you are able to attend. This would require you to maintain good relationships with colleagues by helping them out, but also with the rota manager. It is also about making sure that you leave work on time. This can be achieved by working closely with colleagues and building an efficient handover process so that you are not delayed unnecessarily.

QUESTION 6

Describe a time where you had to defend your own beliefs with regard to the treatment of a patient. What did you do and what was the outcome?

First Impression

Another question following the STAR system, where the question leads you through the structure. The topic is slightly unusual and may scare some people but if you stop one minute to think about it, there is nothing difficult about handling it. The main issue may be for those who are very junior to find an appropriate example.

How to handle the question?

1 – Think about the context in which you may have to defend your beliefs with regard to the treatment of patient.

This could be for example:

- A situation where you made a decision that was queried by one of your peers, or seniors or a nurse, and where you had to defend your views.

- A situation where your decision or belief with regard to treatment was queried either by the patient or one his/her relatives.

- A case review meeting where you were asked to justify your actions.

- A disciplinary environment (I would not recommend that you go there!)

Taking this first generalised step should help you recollect situations where this has happened. Once you have come up with an example, try to remember the various steps that were involved in the story.

2 – Think about the attributes that the question is testing and those that you want to present.

- It is a question about <u>defending</u> your beliefs, therefore it will involve a lot of communication. This question is partly about presenting information in a clear manner in order to convince someone.

- Because you are effectively debating with someone over whether your approach was right or not, you will need to take on board their comments to see if they make sense to you. Your answer will therefore involve an amount of listening.

- If you have to defend your beliefs, it is most likely that you are being criticised or are being placed under pressure. This question is partly about coping with pressure and your ability to keep your cool.

- As a doctor, you should have confidence in your own abilities without demonstrating arrogance or being over-confident (in which case you may not be safe as you are unlikely to check your facts and call for help if required). In your answer you should therefore seek to demonstrate that you are safe by taking a logical approach in resolving the issue at stake. That approach really depends on the situation that you are facing.

3 – Think generally speaking about how you would normally try to convince someone that your judgement is correct.

- First you would ensure that you have all the information to hand to be able to present a sensible case.

- Secondly, you would present your logical arguments to the other person and would wait for their reaction. You would then pay attention to what they have to say, giving them the opportunity to express their opinion freely without interrupting. It will make them feel valued and, you never know, they may have a valid point.

- Thirdly, if your first approach did not work, you may want to try a different approach. This could be either a different way of communication (for example by using a diagram rather than words, or by giving someone a

leaflet to read before you can have your next conversation, etc). In some cases, the alternative approach may be to involve a senior colleague into the debate to give more weight to your argument.

- If none of this works then there may not be an easy conclusion to the problem. If patients are involved, this could involve the complaints procedure, court action etc. For the purpose of answering this question you should ensure that you choose an example where you were successful at defending your beliefs otherwise you will run into trouble, however justified your actions were.

Be careful, in situations of emergency, it may not always be possible to discuss everything for a long time (in fact it may be unsafe and/or negligent to spend too long discussing matters if the patient is not being handled in his best interest. If you discuss an emergency situation, you should ensure that you demonstrate that you have taken every possible step to get input from your seniors if needed, that you acted in line with your best judgement and in the best interest of the patient, and that you have spent time after the event to sort out the conflict.

Example of an effective answer

I had admitted a patient for ketoacidosis who, according to my best judgement, required a high dose of insulin. I asked a staff nurse to administer the treatment, which she refused to do since she would only go ahead with a dose that followed the normal sliding scale.

I spent a couple of minutes explaining patiently and in a normal tone of voice to the nurse, that as well as the patient's blood sugar we needed to deal with the ketosis and the acidosis, which required a high level of insulin. As she refused to go ahead and, in view of the urgency of the situation, I administered the treatment myself in order to ensure the patient was safe at all times.

Once the patient was stabilised, I asked the nurse if she wanted to discuss the matter in a more relaxed setting. Over a cup of coffee in the mess I asked her to explain how she saw the situation and she explained that she had never come across such a situation in the past and did not feel comfortable taking orders without understanding them. I listened attentively to what she had to say, realising that her behaviour could be potentially dangerous for patients.

45

I then spent some time explaining in some detail but in simple terms the facts on diabetic ketoacidosis and why a high dose was necessary. I also explained to her in a non-judgemental manner how her actions may have endangered the patient, emphasising that this should in no way stop her from raising her concerns if she felt she needed to in future.

The nurse felt that she understood the situation better and apologised for her action. This incident enabled us to have a closer relationship and as a result enhanced the standard of care that we were able to provide to all future patient.

Note the emphasis on the communication aspect of the scenario about listening, being non-judgemental but also assertive. Also note that there is some clinical content, however it has been reduced to what is strictly necessary to understand the context and the actions of the individuals involved.

Final Comments

Don't be afraid to go into some detail. Detail and facts will help build up your credibility and will make the example look real. But always make sure that those details are relevant to the question being asked.

You can use the "Outcome" or "Result" section to explain a little bit more than what happened at the end of the story, by adding a sentence about how it helped you become a better doctor. In this example, it is about building bridges with the nurse and enhancing the working relationship. It helps add depth to the answer.

Other questions looking for similar types of answers include:

- Give an example of a situation at work where a patient has not agreed with your diagnosis or management?

QUESTION 7

Describe a time when you had to use creative thinking to solve a problem at work. What did you do and what was the result?

First Impression

Scary! The skill being tested is fairly obvious. The main problem is: what is creative thinking? But again the familiar STAR structure.

How to handle the question?

1 – Ask yourself what the word "creative" means.

The word "creative" refers to the fact that you have used your imagination and initiative to come up with a solution. The question therefore relates to a situation with which you were unfamiliar and for which you had to use your brain power to derive a sensible and effective solution.

2 – Identify the type of situations that you have faced, where you were exposed to an unusual problem.

This may include situations where:

- You had to deal with a patient who presented with a condition that you were unfamiliar with.

- Your senior asked you to organise something that you had never organised before (educational meeting, audit project, rota, etc).

- You had to deal with several tasks at the same time, which looked completely impossible to you at the time (for example routine work and several emergencies all at the same time).

3 – Identify the skills that you can demonstrate in your example.

This is a question about what you would do in a situation where you have a problem that has no obvious solution to you. Things you can do include:

- Asking for help from seniors (although this is not really creative by itself!)

- Looking things up in a textbook (already more proactive) or on Medline/Cochrane etc (evidence-based practice is popular at the moment!)

- Discussing issues with colleagues/seniors (team work is always appreciated!)

- Using all the resources available to you, delegating work to the appropriate people (even better!)

- Using a different communication approach (see question 4).

4 – Find an example that suits you best and would enable you to demonstrate your ability to handle unusual situation using several tools.

Here are a few examples that should enable you to think of your own:

- You have a patient who looks like he has a particular condition but something tells you that there is more to it than meets the eye. Your creative thinking leads you to do some reading in textbooks and on the internet, before having a chat with your Registrar. You also feel that another doctor from another ward can help, so you contact them and arrange a discussion on the patient's condition to find a solution to your problem.

- You work in a hospital where the rota is imposing too many constraints on junior doctors (perhaps they have made a mess of implementing the European Working Time Directive). You come up with a solution of your own, discuss it with your colleagues and then arrange a meeting with a consultant to discuss the problems caused by the current system and to offer your own ideas. As a result your proposal is implemented.

- You are running a clinic where you constantly have the same problem with patients. For example there is some simple information that they need to take away with them after the clinic but that information often gets scribbled on a piece of paper, which they lose. You take the initiative to produce a proforma slip which doctors can complete quickly by ticking the right boxes and which patients are less likely to ignore.

- You have discovered that members of your team often forget to consider certain points in their history taking, which slows down patient management and may lead to errors. You know that the current system has been implemented by one of the consultants who thinks that it works well and you therefore need to convince everyone that the system needs to be changed. Your creative thinking leads you to use diplomacy and tact to highlight the issue and to offer a counter-solution without upsetting the consultant in question.

- You are on-call, facing a difficult case, and none of your seniors are available for help. You can then describe the research you did to find a solution and how you used other resources available (nurses' advice, other SHOs/seniors from other wards) to solve your problem.

Final Comments

When you write your answer, make sure you follow the STAR approach. Conclude on a personal note. In this question you can mention how the situation helped you gain confidence in your own abilities to handle complex situations or how it made you realise how important it was to use the resources available to you and to work as a team.

Questions revolving around this theme include:

- Describe a time when you had to think beyond the obvious to manage a patient's health. What did you do and what was the outcome?

- Describe a time when you made your workplace more efficient. How did you plan and organise this?

QUESTION 8

Outline a situation when you demonstrated professional integrity as a doctor. What happened? What did you do and what was the outcome?

First Impression

Integrity is not an easy concept to define. Once you have clarified what integrity means, you should have no problem finding an example.

How to approach the question?

1 – Think about what integrity means in your day to day work

Integrity refers to your ability to do the right thing when faced with a situation that it would be easy to ignore because it makes your life easier. This may be:

- Situations where you have made a mistake, where you would be expected to own up to it and take corrective action.

- Situations where you should know how to handle particular issue but somehow you don't. Integrity is about admitting your deficiency and working towards addressing it (a lack of integrity would be pretending that you know what to do, which may put your patients and colleagues at risk).

- Situations where you discover that something is wrong and where you take proactive steps to address the situation (for example, if you discover that one of your colleagues has made a mistake, is an alcoholic, takes drugs, has abused a patient or is underperforming/incompetent).

- Situations where you were pressurised into doing something that you knew or felt was wrong and where you resisted the pressure (e.g. a relative, a friend or a colleague encouraging you to breach patient confidentiality).

- Colleague who wants a "favour" that would place you in a difficult position, (covering up for a mistake they made, prescribing them controlled drugs, etc.)

There are other situations where you can demonstrate integrity but they do not always lend themselves well to examples. For instance, finding a wallet in the street and taking it back to its owner would be an example of integrity but
(i) it is not exactly medical;
(ii) it is too basic to be worthy of interest when it comes to writing 250 words on the subject.

How to structure your answer?

As ever, since they are asking for a specific example, follow the STAR structure, making sure that you focus on a particular event. Because you need to talk about your integrity, you first need to explain the context that forced you to choose the integrity route.

Example of the relatives exercising pressure to breach confidentiality.

- If you want to talk about a relative who wanted you to release information about the patient, you should explain what the patient's condition was, why they did not want their relatives to know anything, and why the relatives were pressurising you.

- In the "Action" section you can then describe how you handled the relatives (think about the communication skills - listening, showing understanding, empathy) and how you felt you needed to stand up to them. If needed, you can also explain how you called a senior colleague to put more weight on your argument. You can also talk about what was happening with the patient at that time and how you handled the communication with them in that context.

- To conclude, you should explain how through good communication, team playing and gentle assertiveness you managed to resolve a potentially explosive situation.

Example of the mistake that you made and admitted to.

- Make sure you choose a situation where the patient wasn't placed in a dangerous/unsafe situation – there is no need for it in this question since the focus is on how you admitted to the mistake rather than the mistake itself.

- Describe what you had been asked to do (Task).

- Explain the mistake that you made, sticking to the essential (not too much clinical information). Also explain why you made the mistake (is it because you were inexperienced or had misunderstood what you had been asked to do, or some other reason?). Do not be too shy, everyone makes mistakes. Just make sure yours wasn't a deadly or potentially deadly one!

- Explain how you identified that you had made the mistake and what you did after that. Things you can detail include:

  ➤ Remedying it straight away if it was a simple mistake.

  ➤ Going to your seniors either for help to sort things out, or to report that you made a mistake.

  ➤ Taking every single step possible to sort the matter out.

  ➤ Discussing the issue with colleagues and particularly how you will handle the communication with the patient, if a patient was involved.

  ➤ Apologising to the relevant people (colleagues, patients, relatives, etc)

  ➤ Critical Incident Form if required

- Conclude your story by describing how everyone reacted in the end (patient/colleagues happy, etc) and what you learnt from the example (this could be that you learnt how a simple apology can go a long way, or how admitting your mistake early meant that the problem could be resolved quickly.

Final Comments

In this case, the word "Integrity" actually featured in the text of the question. Integrity can also be tested as part of a more specific scenario. In particular they could force you to focus on one of the scenarios listed above by asking you the following questions:

- Provide an example of situation where you made a mistake.

- Describe a time where you failed to manage a patient effectively. What did you do, how did you resolve the situation?

- How would you react if one of your colleagues asked you to do something you felt was inappropriate.

- How would you react if you suspected one of your colleagues had a drink or drugs problem? (See question 16 for more details on this)

For the first two questions (example of a mistake, failure to manage a patient effectively), the answer is pretty much as per the previous page. You need to demonstrate that you recognised that you did wrong, admitted to it and then sought to resolve the matter as swiftly as possible. You also need to discuss the communication implications with both the patient and your colleagues, and what you learnt as a result.

For the others, the question is not actually asking for an example but is asking for a pattern of general behaviour you would demonstrate in a hypothetical situation. These questions are easier to formulate (they don't need to follow the STAR system since there is no story to tell) but they require you to think carefully about all the issues involved and to present them in a logical manner.

QUESTION 9

Describe a time when you had to obtain informed consent from a patient who was in a vulnerable position. How did you communicate with them, which strategies did you use and what was the outcome?

First Impression

It looks like a question on how to seek consent so most candidates will rush into describing how they can seek consent. Don't make the same mistake; the question is more complex than it looks.

The clue is in the second part of the question "How did you communicate with them". It is a communication question, and more precisely, a question about how to communicate in a challenging situation i.e. where you will have to think carefully about how you will need to approach the problem (clue: creative thinking!). The consent-seeking context is just a platform to make your job easier in finding an example. In your answer, you will need to make a clever mix of the three aspects: seeking consent, communication and creative/lateral thinking.

How to approach the question

1 – Identify vulnerable patients you have encountered.
This could include:

- Patients who are elderly, of sound mind but easily influenced.
- Patients who have psychiatric problems.
- Patients who may be making decisions against their own best interest because of some other factors (fear to become a burden on relatives, etc).
- Patients who have just had bad news broken to them.

You can then more easily identify which patient would be a suitable candidate for a good example.

2 – Follow a logical structure, taking the approach chronologically.
Here again (hopefully by now you have got the idea about this!), the STAR system needs to be followed.

- Start by explaining the context. Who was the patient (ensuring you give enough detail to show how/why they were vulnerable) and what did you need to seek their consent for?

- Detail how you sought consent (explaining things slowly, checking their understanding, drawing diagrams if needed etc) but throughout your answer explain how their vulnerability impacted on your actions and how you resolved each problem that this presented you with.

- For example, simply saying "I explained the procedure in simple terms" is too weak because this could apply to anyone, not just a vulnerable patient. Instead you could write something along the lines of "I explained the procedure in simple terms, using a diagram to illustrate my words, but the patient seemed a bit confused about some of the detail and was taking a long time to understand some of the basic information. I therefore asked the nurse and also one of the relatives to explain in their own words what I had described, which helped the patient along."

- As another example, instead of saying "the patient was crying so I gave her some leaflets and asked her to come back later", which sounds harsh, you need to explain why you acted in that way and show that you used a sensitive approach that matched the distress of the patient. This could give an answer like "As the patient was crying uncontrollably, I spent some time gently reassuring her that we would do our best for her and asked her if she was okay to continue or wanted to go home. I offered her the opportunity to study some leaflets and come back at a later stage, which she gratefully accepted. She returned three days later etc etc"

- Try not to go too technical on the "seeking consent" aspect as it is not really the aim of the question. The only really important aspects for these questions are:

  ➤ Explaining the procedure in detail in a clear manner, including pros, cons, alternatives, risks (no need to go into detail in these questions)
  ➤ Checking the understanding of the patient and answering their questions.

➢ Reassuring the patient they can change their mind and can take the time to think about their decision

▪ In some cases you may need to address the competence of the patient, which you may have assessed by asking a psychiatrist to review the patient or asking for senior advice.

Final Comments

It is important to recognise when an answer looks as if it is about a given topic when in fact it is asking you to concentrate on totally different skills, simply using that topic as a platform for discussion. In this example, it would have been too easy to consider the consent issue whilst totally ignoring the communication challenges posed by a vulnerable person.

Make sure you spend some time analysing the question properly. There is nothing worse than realising after 20 minutes that you have wasted your time and that you need to start again.

QUESTION 10

Describe a time when you felt annoyed and frustrated but had to hide this emotion in order to deal successfully with a patient. What did you do afterwards do deal with your emotions?

First Impression

A slightly different type of topic, no longer asking you how you used your skills to achieve a result, but asking you about your own feelings and how you dealt with them. This is good if you are someone who opens up easily. If you are of the shy type or if you come from a background where expressing your emotions is not the norm, then you may need a little bit more preparation.

Otherwise, it is yet another example and this should trigger your Pavlovian reflex: STAR with a specific situation.

How to handle the question

1 – Ask yourself why you might be annoyed or frustrated when dealing with the patient.

It may be because of a personal issue or because something happened between you and a colleague. But there would be little interest in talking about such a situation. If this were what they wanted they would simply ask the question in a more direct manner.

The question therefore refers to the fact that the patient him/herself will have annoyed you or frustrated you. Think of situations where patients may have had that effect on you. This may be because:

- They are lying to you.

- They keep coming back with the same problem but never take the advice that you give them.

- They won't go for your recommendation and are asking for non-conventional treatments that appear futile.

- They are difficult to take a history from (not giving clear facts, hiding things, etc).

- They have lifestyles and behaviours that are detrimental to their health and fail to realise this or fail to attempt to modify their behaviour (e.g. smoking whilst pregnant).

- They are hypochondriacs and are wasting your time.

- They are rude, impatient or demanding.

- They think they know better than the doctor (e.g. from information they obtained on the internet or simply their own arrogance).

2 - Pick a good example from your past and ask yourself how you reacted to that patient.
In your description of events, you will need to explain what the patient was doing or saying that annoyed you, how it made you feel, what you did to keep your cool and how you handled the conversation with the patient. Try to be descriptive and explain not just what you did, but also why you did it i.e. what you were hoping to achieve.

For example, if you said "The patient kept repeating that he knew what was wrong with him; I let him talk and then explained that he would still require a referral to the specialist consultant", you would be merely stating the facts. These may represent a suitable approach in view of the situation that you were facing but they are not very descriptive of what was going on in your mind (remember, this is all about feelings and how annoyed you were!).

You could address this by wording your answer slightly differently, for example as follows: "The patient kept repeating that he knew what was wrong with him when it was clear he was on the wrong track. I found his attitude annoying but rather than risking irritating him by confronting him with the reality, I let him talk with a view to develop his confidence in me through listening and by nodding occasionally to signal that I was showing an interest in his story.

Letting him talk also enabled me to collect my thoughts on the situation, to find a different angle from which I could approach him etc."

When you describe the situation, you should obviously concentrate on the manner with which you interacted with the patient and dealt with your frustration at the time. Don't forget that you can get help from colleagues too!

3 – Make sure you address the final part of the question,
Many candidates often address one part of the question and forget about the rest, either because they are simply not concentrating or because they are not sure how to handle it. The last part is asking what you did afterwards to deal with your emotions. In such situations where you have to deal with frustration, there are really only two things you can do:

- Discuss the situation with colleagues.

- Have a change of scene. Do something different like going for a walk, playing a sport, meeting with friends and talk about your day, spending time with your family, and simply relax.

It also won't harm to discuss how you learnt from the situation and to mention that you are now better equipped to deal with the type of situations that you are describing.

Final Comments
In questions such as these, where the emphasis is not so much on the facts but on the feelings that you have encountered, you must try to get into a habit of describing the situation, how it made you feel and how you reacted to that feeling. This will then prompt a reaction from the patient, which will make you feel something else and again you will react to it. This will take you through the story in a natural fashion, thus ensuring that you address the question at the right level.

QUESTION 11

Why do you want to become a GP?

First Impression

"Oh no.... I never know how to answer this question." People are scared of this question for several reasons:

- They've never really thought about it.
- They don't really want to become a GP but it's a nice enough job.
- The only reason they want to become GP is because it pays well and there are no jobs anywhere else but they know they shouldn't say that.
- They know roughly what they should be saying but don't know how to.

How to approach this question

1 – Think about what you actually think about why you want to be a GP.
Too many people get stuck in answering this question because they simply haven't thought about it. Objectively speaking there are many reasons why doctors want to become GPs (other than money):

- **Holistic approach:** as a GP you do not only deal with physical issues but also with psychological and social issues.

- **Continuity of care:** unlike most hospital specialties, GPs see their patients throughout their life and not just for one particular condition. They are effectively managing their patients' health over the long-term.

- **Close contact with patients:** GPs can build long term relationships with patients. This close contact allows them to have a better understanding of their patients. As well as doctors, they can also act as counsellors.

- **Exposure to a variety of specialties:** a GP deals with all ages from neonatal/paediatrics to elderly cases and manages patients with various conditions, including chronic, acute and emergencies.

- **Variety in the type of activities undertaken:** a GP does not just handle patients in clinics, he does home visits, gets involved in management issues. General Practice also offers an opportunity to become involved in prevention work.

- **Early responsibilities:** GPs have a greater responsibility for patient care much earlier on in their career than would be possible in a hospital. Also, since GPs are working in small businesses, each doctor takes on more responsibilities and can get involved early on in managerial issues.

- **Possibility to subspecialise:** GPs can now subspecialise. This is a great opportunity to combine specialist expertise with the advantages of GP practice (especially if you have worked for some time in a specialty)

- **Opportunity to work in broader teams:** GPs are involved with the community at large. This includes their immediate colleagues at the surgery and hospital doctors in secondary care settings. It also includes social workers, physiotherapists, nutritionists, community nurses, etc.

- **Flexibility of lifestyle/ Greater work-life balance:** Do not be afraid of mentioning this. In fact they will expect you to do so. It is an important part of life as a GP.

2 – Make sure that you use a very clear structure in your answer.
Whatever you do, make sure that you address at least FIVE of the points above as part of the marking system revolves around the number of reasons that you have.

Once you have determined the points that you find most attractive, you need to present them in a structured manner. You can either adopt a simple but effective list structure where you have a short heading and a paragraph for each point that you want to discuss (a bit in the style of the list above), or you can adopt a free-style format, with maybe 3 or 4 paragraphs which each deal with one or two reasons. Either way the content should not be that different, whichever format you adopt.

Please note that if you are not very good at writing nice prose, you would be better off adopting a bullet point approach as it will clearly lay out your ideas and it will not require you to make nice transitions between the different paragraphs.

3 – Explain why each of the reasons that you quote are important to you
As you can imagine, the above reasons are more or less quoted by every single applicant in one order or another. It is therefore important that you are able to personalise your answer by relating it to your experience and explaining what you mean by it.

For example (using the list approach):

Holistic approach
As an SHO in Elderly Care I gained much satisfaction from dealing with the psychological and social issues of my patients when discussing their conditions or preparing discharge plans. As a GP I will be able to extend this global standard of care to all my patients.

Greater work/life balance
As a young mother of a two-year old child, I feel it is important to spend time with my family whilst simultaneously building a successful career for myself. A career in General Practice will help me achieve the right balance between these two important elements of my life.

Exposure to various specialties
In my current post I enjoy dealing with cardiac patients as much as I enjoyed managing psychiatric, O&G, respiratory and oncology patients in the past. As a GP I will be able to maintain my interest and expertise in all specialties, thus providing me with a diverse and enriching career.

Note: You can see that the list approach is very effective in pushing your message across with a main heading and a short explanation. I would only recommend the traditional free-style approach if you have a good command of English and are able to write an impressive essay on yourself, or if the question imposes it.

Final Comments

Try to choose 5 items that cover a range of subjects (patient, management, personal life, etc). Look at the number of words that the recruiters require for the whole question and divide it by 5. A total answer requiring 250 words will correspond to 50 words per topic that you want to address. To give you an idea, the three paragraphs written on the previous page have the following number of words:

- "Holistic approach" : 49 words
- "Work/life balance": 51 words.
- "Exposure to various specialties": 54 words.

As you can see you do not need to write much information to comply with the rules and write an effective answer. You simply need to be very selective. Words go quickly when you have a lot to say!

Obviously, if you are asked to write an essay in 500 words, you can double the size of each paragraph. You can achieve this by:

- adding more information about how you have gained an interest in the feature that you are describing and expanding a little on your experience.

- discussing more features. There are nine features listed above so you can easily expand on the five that you have originally chosen. If you choose to do this, you may wish to group together some of the features, so that you do not end up with 9 different paragraphs. For example, "Close contact with patients" and "Continuity of care" can be grouped. So can "Variety of specialties" and "Variety of activities".

Warning

This question is not phrased to mean "Describe how you have discovered that General Practice was the career for you". In other words you do not have to write your entire life story. This is particularly important if you have a career that has been geared towards one specialty only (like O&G) so far as, if you approach the "Why GP" question by discussing your career progression, you will find yourself discussing your one-sided experience in too much detail.

QUESTION 12

What personal attributes do you have that would make you a good GP?

First Impression

Easy question since all the qualities can be found in the person specification. But not so easy to write about in a way that differentiates you from the others. You will need to think hard about your personal experience to write a good and complete answer to this question,

How to approach this question

1 – Choose a handful of attributes that cover a broad range of skills
Examples include:

- Commitment to keeping up to date. Interest in personal and professional development.

- Good communication skills including being a good listener, able to show empathy, able to express yourself clearly and in a way that is adapted to your audience.

- Good team player. Get on well with people, participate actively to the team effort, willing to help others and seek help from them.

- Having a life.

- Good managerial and organisational skills. Able to prioritise your work, to use the resources available to you adequately. Able to deal with pressure within your work through good time management and good relationships with others.

- Confident in your abilities and able to use your knowledge and training to resolve cases and problems through your initiative. At the same time, a safe doctor who is able to recognise their limitations and their mistakes.

There are many other ways of presenting the skills of a GP, and there are other skills you can present too. Make sure you familiarise yourself with the person specification.

2 – Choose an adequate structure.

As for Question 11 (Why GP?) you can choose the list approach where you simply name the quality that you have, followed by a paragraph that contains the related text. This should give you one paragraph per skill, each of which has a clear heading. The advantage of this structure is that the reader can immediately identify your main messages without having to read a whole load of text. It is also much easier to write because you don't have to make transitions. They are asking for a list, you give them a list; it's as simple as that.

Alternatively you may want to write an answer that is based on an essay format, provided you are able to make it hold together well. Essay-type answers do not highlight the message in such an obvious manner but they can be very effective and impressive if your command of English is good.

Generally speaking, unless the question forces you to write an essay, I would recommend that you take the list approach (sometimes also referred to as the bullet point approach). It is also a recommendation made by many GP trainers that I have talked to.

3 – Personalise your answer.

Simply listing the skills will take you nowhere since most candidates will know what they are and will also list them in the same way as you. For each skill you should give examples that demonstrate that you indeed have the skill, taking care to bring into your answer your personal experience. For example:

I am a good listener and treat my patients with empathy.
As an SHO in O&G I often dealt with distraught mother who had lost their baby. I spent time reassuring them and providing the moral and psychological support they needed. I also often had to deal with teenage pregnancies where being a good listener was crucial in helping me build a good rapport with the patient.

> **I am organised and have good time management skills.**
> Having worked on several busy wards I have gained experience of time management, making task lists, prioritising my work appropriately and working with my colleagues to ensure that I deliver a high standard of clinical care. As an A&E SHO I learnt to work efficiently under pressure, which has equipped me well for life as a GP.

Final Comments

Such a question should not come as a total surprise to you. So make sure you have prepared yourself well beforehand.

Candidates find this question scary because they are looking at it as one big block instead of a series of smaller modules. All you really need to do is select 5 or 6 skills you want to address and write a short paragraph of 50 to 60 words for each, using your personal experience. Once you have done this preliminary work, you can use these modules to answer other questions too.

QUESTION 13

Describe a clinical situation where you have used a holistic approach in managing a patient. What patient needs were identified and how did you personally address these?

First Impression

The aim of the question is clear: discuss the holistic approach through a real-life scenario. The needs to be identified are also clear since they are part of the holistic approach: physical, social, psychological. No real surprise there.

The key to this question is really to find a good example that enables you to demonstrate your experience of all three aspects, all this with one single patient.

Note: the question asks for a clinical situation. It does not mean you have to go hardcore on clinical information but simply that it must be related to a patient at work, rather than, say, a friend whom you might have dealt with.

How to approach the question

1 – Identify a particular patient with whom you had to deal with not only their condition but also their psychological and social needs.
This could include:

- An elderly patient who needed to be discharged.

- A patient to whom you broke bad news.

- A homeless patient

- A patient with multiple conditions ranging from psychological to physical.

2 – Use a simple structure for your answer.

This question asks for an example and you should therefore follow the STAR structure. The "Action" section is more or less dictated by the wording of the question.

Situation/Task

Describe what type of patient it was, how they presented to you.

Action

Explain that you understood there were several aspects that needed to be dealt with, from a physical perspective as well as a psychosocial point of view. You can then take all these needs in turn in a very structured manner

- Describe the *physical needs* of the patients and how you addressed them. In this section try to give just enough detail to give a good impression that you were competent but do not overdo it on the clinical detail – this is not the purpose of the question. In some cases, your answers could even be as simple as referring the patient to a specialist or to a senior colleague. All that matters is that you have addressed the needs in a sensible manner.

- Describe the *social needs* of the patient. Did they live on their own? Did they have family? Could their family cope with the burden? Did they need care in the community? What about financial aspects? Did they need advice about claiming benefits? Were there charities that could help? Did their home require special adjustments? Did you enlist the help of some members of the multidisciplinary team to sort out some of the issues (care workers, occupational therapist, community nurses, etc)? Did you provide leaflets? Etc

- Describe the *psychological needs* of the patient. Did they need counseling? Did they require a referral to a psychiatrist? Did you arrange for the patient to get in touch with charities? Did you spend some time counseling them yourself? Did you address this issue with the relatives? Did the relatives need counseling too?

Result
Explain how the patient was helped with your approach (grateful, much improved lifestyle, got a new job and sorted themselves out, etc).

Final Comment

Don't be afraid to go into detail in this question. They are asking for it! Make sure you allocate equal weight to the three aspects and, if you can, separate them out so that the reader can quickly identify that you have thought about the whole picture.

Try to be as practical as you can, describing what you physically did to address the patient's needs. Too many candidates write sentences such as "I identified the patient's psychological needs and addressed them appropriately". This only explains what needs you identified, but it would be nice to know what those needs exactly were and how they were addressed. For example the patient may have had a need for psychological support and consequently you discussed support groups and you gave the patient leaflets to read and website addresses to visit.

This question is easier than others because its aim is clearly stated: they want to test your holistic approach to a patient. Other questions may call for a demonstration of the holistic in a more disguised manner. See Question 14.

QUESTION 14

You are asked to inform a patient that they have carcinoma of the colon, What issues does this raise for you?

First Impression

Many people would be jumping with joy on seeing this question, proclaiming "I know how to break bad news". The truth is, once you start thinking closely about the question, it is about more than just breaking bad news. It is also about the holistic approach and your ability to cover all the angles that are relevant to the patient.

Secondly, note that this question is not asking for an example (since not many people have actually encountered such a specific situation). Therefore you can take a more free-style approach.

How to approach the question

1 – Spend a few minutes brainstorming the issues.
First there are two people (mainly) in this conversation: the patient and you.

The patient
You will need to address his/her needs (physical, social, psychological). You will also need to ensure he/she is handled carefully during the consultation when you break the bad news.

You
You must be prepared for the consultation by having all the facts to hand and have a clear idea of what you will be telling the patient, how you will address his needs and how you will communicate with him. You should also make sure that you are prepared psychologically for the consultation, as it may be hard on you.

2 – Think about the situation that they are asking for. Why have they asked for carcinoma of the colon and not generally about any other disease?

Colon Carcinoma is a disease that is curable and there are several options for this (surgery, chemo etc). Again do not fall into the trap of going hardcore on the clinical aspect – it is not the point of the question – but somewhere you will need to mention that you will need to refer the patient to an appropriate specialist.

Colon Carcinoma is also a disease that could have a big impact on the patient. If the patient needs a colostomy bag, he will need psychological support not only to deal with the bad news itself but also with the consequences it will have on his/her lifestyle. It may also impact on his ability to earn money. For example if his job involves a lot of physical activity, a colostomy bag may mean the end to his employment, his ability to provide for his family, etc. This will have a social impact.

3 – Breaking the news
As mentioned earlier it would be easy to misinterpret this question as being solely about breaking bad news. However you cannot ignore completely this aspect of the question, although you should stick to the minimum (bearing in mind that there are plenty of other issues you really want to talk about).

The main skills that you want to demonstrate are that you are able to prepare yourself adequately for the meeting and that you will be able to put the patient at ease. This will include mentioning that you will arrange for a long consultation slot so that you have time to address all the issues, that you will arrange for your phone/bleep to be diverted so as not to be interrupted, that you may ask a nurse to sit with you for the patient's support and your own, maybe ask the patient to bring a relative along. You should also mention that you will check the patient's understanding and will give him/her time to react to the news as well as opportunities to ask questions.

4 – Structure your answer

Because the question is only asking for the issues that it raises with you, you can, if you prefer, provide the information in a list format rather than an essay format, developing each heading as you go along. The main issues you should raise are:

Your own preparation

- Ensure that you familiarise yourself with the results and understand the implications. You will need to be fully familiar with the options in order to inform the patient accordingly and to be able to answer his questions. This may require you to speak to other professionals such as a colorectal surgeon or an oncologist.

- Read up on the disease. Gather any documentation that you could give the patient (Leaflets, website addresses, details of charities, etc)

- Prepare yourself psychologically to break the news. It could be hard if you know the patient well for example. To help, you could ask a nurse to sit with you (she will also be useful to support the patient when you break the news).

- Prepare yourself for the patient's reaction.

Making the patient feel at ease / Consultation set-up.

- Ensure that you allow sufficient time for the consultation. There is a lot to discuss and the patient will need his own time to react and ask questions. This may take the equivalent of a few appointments.

- If possible ask the patient to come accompanied so that they can benefit from their own support network. In some cases, you may need to visit the patient at home if you feel it would be more beneficial (for example if someone is vulnerable and cannot be accompanied, or has mobility problems)

- Ensure you are free of disturbances by asking someone else to handle all calls and letting the secretaries know that you should be left alone.

Breaking the news
- Explain to the patient what has happened so far, dropping hints about the diagnostic. Gauge their reaction and adapt your speed and delivery accordingly.

- Provide as much detail as they want to hear, give them the time to react and make sure you cover the spectrum of issues to be addressed.

Physical needs of the patient
- Inform the patient about the possibilities open to him/her, whether surgical or medical (or palliative in the extreme cases).

- Explain you will refer them to the appropriate specialist so that they can be dealt with as well as possible.

Psychological needs of the patient
- Review the information that you have about their past, gauge how they are reacting at the time of the consultation and determine the level of support they may require. They should get support from you through any follow-up appointment, from their family (you will need to discuss with them the extent to which the family can help), from external organisations such as support groups or charities such as Macmillan nurses, full details of which you should provide to the patient.

Social needs of the patient
- Discuss with the patient the implications of the disease on his lifestyle, his job, his family. Does he/she require help? You may need to involve social services and carers. Does he/she need help with benefits or his financial situation in general (especially if he/she was the main bread winner).

The relatives
- Try to identify how the relatives will cope from a physical and psychological point of view and whether they require assistance too.

- For carcinoma of the colon, you may also want to carry out some generic testing to determine whether they are at risk of developing the disease too.

<u>**Ending the consultation**</u>

- Give the patient all the leaflets and information they require to make whatever decision they have to make and to contact the relevant organisations.

- Arrange for any referral you have to make and reassure the patient you will do whatever is possible to help them out.

- Arrange a follow-up consultation to determine the progress made by the patient and identify any physical, psychological or social issues that may have arisen as a result of the initial management step.

Final Comments

As you can see there is quite a lot you can make out of an innocent question on breaking bad news. As a rule of thumb, if the question looks simple then it probably isn't! Take a step back and have a mini-brainstorm to identify if there are other issues that you can address and that the recruiters may be looking for.

QUESTION 15

You have been asked to organise a weekly educational meeting for your colleagues. How would you approach this task?

First Impression

A relatively easy question too if you can demonstrate your ability to think laterally and to use all the resources available to you.

When this question was asked in 2005 by the Scottish deaneries, many people found it difficult to answer it because "they had never organised a meeting before". In reality, if you think carefully about the skills that are being tested and use your logic you should be able to provide a complete answer without much of a problem (In the same way that for Question 14 you did not need to have broken bad news for colon carcinoma to have an idea of how you should approach the situation).

How to handle the question

Think about what the question may be looking for. It is not really testing if you can organise a meeting; everyone can send an email to ask people. The issue is really: are you able to think about the different aspects of the meeting and how you can make it successful in relation to its aims?

- What is your objective? To organise a meeting that people will want to go to, otherwise you are wasting your time.

- It is a weekly meeting (don't forget this aspect! There is a big difference between organising a one-off event and organising a regular event). Therefore you will need to make sure that your colleagues want to attend every week! It had better be good and you will need to make them feel involved.

- If it is a weekly meeting, there is no way you can do all the work by yourself. You will need to arrange for different speakers and you will need to get the logistics sorted out (booking a room, photocopying the handouts, drinks, maybe sponsorship). After all you need to work sometimes. So you will need to get help from someone. Also you may not be an expert at booking rooms and catering.

- You will need to make sure people can attend; therefore your meeting will need to be at a convenient time.

Essentially before you can start organising the meeting you will need a lot of information that you will need to get from other people. You will also need other people to help you out (unless you fancy sending all the emails every week and doing the photocopying yourself!) Hence it is also a question about management and teamwork.

How to structure the answer to the question

Take a step by step approach to the meeting:

Defining the meeting

1 – Because it is a weekly meeting you will need to find new topics every week as well as new presenters. In order to ensure the success of your project and to ensure that your colleagues get as much as they can out of the meetings, you would approach them and ask them what type of topics would interest them, when is the most suitable time for them and whether there are subjects that they may wish to present themselves. This can be done either face to face or via a simple questionnaire that they can complete. *(Involving team members, addressing your colleagues' needs)*

2 – You will also probably need to involve some of your senior colleagues who may have their own ideas about what the meeting should achieve. They may also have ideas that would make your life easier. *(Seeking help when appropriate / Using the resources available)*

3 – Once you have gathered some basic information about the type of topics your colleagues want to discuss and what the seniors are aiming for, you can start putting together a document that summarises your findings and that you can discuss with your consultant. The two of you can then settle on a format and an appropriate time. *(Team work)*

4 – You may also wish to discuss with your seniors whether you should limit the meeting to your immediate colleagues or whether it should be open to other departments, and even other professions (nurses, secretaries, etc) in the team. *(Lateral thinking)*

<u>Sorting out the practicalities</u>
5 – Once the meeting has some shape, you will need to ensure that people can attend it. You should probably have a discussion with the rota manager so that they can ensure that the time is protected and that all bleeps are covered appropriately. *(Team work/Organisation)*

6 – You should also liaise with a secretary to ensure that the meeting is advertised appropriately, that a room is booked and that all speakers have been notified of their engagement. *(Team work/Organisation)*

7 – You should be in touch with the speakers regularly to ensure that they are on track (otherwise you will have no meeting) and to arrange for any material to be given in advance (using the secretary for photocopying). For external speakers, you will need to get in touch with them to double check their attendance and coordinate any sponsorship.
Management/Organisation/Team Work)

<u>Running the meeting</u>
8 – Ensure that the meeting is chaired appropriately either by you or someone else, and collect feedback after the meeting so that you can improve for next time. *(Willingness to improve / Team work)*

Final Comments

As you can see, ultimately it is a question about team work and management, and your ability to organise information and people. Once you have identified these features, you can derive a lot of information using common sense.

QUESTION 16

You suspect that one of your colleagues is working whilst under the influence of alcohol. How would you approach the problem? Justify your actions.

First Impression

This is a classic interview question that calls for your common sense as well as your understanding of your duties and responsibilities. The main problem is that the question does not clearly state whether you are to address it in a hospital or a GP context. You can either choose one that you prefer or do both, it does not really matter. The answer is roughly the same either way.

Note the final statement "Justify your actions". This is to stop you simply saying what you would do without explaining what you were trying to achieve by doing it. It is something that you should aim to do without being asked anyway.

How to approach the question

1 – Think about the skills that the question is testing.

- This is about a colleague who is drunk either now or at times. One aspect is therefore the issue of patient safety both immediate and long-term.

- Alcoholism is a serious problem that could lead the doctor to practice with serious consequences. As a junior doctor, you would be wise to ensure that someone senior knows about the problem.

- You colleague has a health problem that may be linked to a sensitive personal situation. You must make sure you handle the situation sensitively and provide him with support if necessary (and/or arrange for him to receive support).

2 – Remind yourself of your duties

According to the duties of a doctor written by the GMC, you have a duty to act quickly to protect patients if you have good reasons to believe that a colleague is not fit to practice. It means you can't wait too long! On the other end, "act quickly" is not really explicitly defined, but you should be able to use your judgement appropriately.

Good medical practice (for those of you who have read the booklet) also says that you should be "willing to deal openly and supportively with problems in the performance, conduct or health of team members". This is an invitation to discuss the situation both with your colleague and with seniors. Beware of the term whistle-blowing. It is rather extreme and does not sound terribly endearing when you are looking to recruit someone who should be able to handle such delicate situation in a sensitive manner.

Read paragraph 27 of "Good Medical Practice". This will give you a clue about the right course of action. Essentially:

- You should share your concerns with an appropriate senior person such as the clinical director, following the Trust procedures.

- If you are still concerned about patient safety (for example because you feel the problem is not being addressed) then you should report the matter to the relevant regulatory body (e.g. royal college).

- If, at any time, you are unsure, seek help from a defense union or the GMC.

As you can see you will find it difficult to answer the question confidently if you have no knowledge of all this. Having said that, you should be able to reproduce most of it through common sense.

3 – Structure your answer

Essentially the above information will give you a clear idea about how the answer should be worded and a clear structure.

Dealing with the immediate patient safety issue
Your main concern should be the safety of the patients.

- If your colleague is working under the influence of alcohol, you should approach him to make sure you are correct. You should be able to detect it without too much problem.

- Explain to your colleague that you feel he has been drinking and that this compromises patient care. Discuss with him the possibility that he should take the rest of the day off. If he accepts then there is no issue, if he refuses then you should contact someone who could convince him, such as your Registrar or Consultant.

- Once your colleague has been sent home, ensure that all the patients he has already seen are reviewed if need be (either by yourself or a colleague) to ensure that that have been dealt with safely.

- You should also liaise with a manager to ensure your colleague's absence is being covered.

Involving seniors
Once you have handled the immediate aspect of patient care, you should ensure their long-term safety and ensure that the problem is in the hands of people who can act and make a difference.

- Look up the procedures in place in your Trust to see what you should do next. They will most likely ask you to contact a senior colleague (as per GMC guidelines).The most obvious person to contact will be your consultant, but you could also go to the Clinical Director if necessary. In a GP practice, this could be a senior GP or the practice manager

- If you feel that the situation is not being addressed successfully and that patients are still in danger then you should act further to protect patients by going to the relevant authorities such as the deanery if it is a junior colleague or the relevant Royal College.

- If you have any doubt about how to proceed, then you can get help from the GMC, or your defence union (MDU, MPS, etc).

Your colleague
▪ Your colleague may have personal problems and, despite the fact that he has been endangering patients' lives (potentially), you should avoid being too judgemental and should offer your support. The level of support that you provide will of course depend on how well you know him and could range from simply being nice and helpful to spending time with him to help him overcome his problem. In any case it will require some flexibility within the team, particularly if the colleague is required to take some time away from clinical duties to sort his problem out.

Final Comment

This question is easy once you have the structure clear in your head. There are easy marks to be picked up provided you can justify your actions.

Make sure you familiarise yourself well with the Good Medical Practice issued by the GMC. You can access it on their website at www.gmc-uk.org. It deals with many aspects of a doctor's responsibilities and often provides valuable information to answer questions on all sorts of topics.

QUESTION 17

Outline a time when you had to support a colleague with a work related problem. What did you do and what was the outcome?

First impression

A good and reasonable question to test your ability to work with others in difficult times. Again, a question asking for an example with the STAR system being explicitly requested in the body of the question. The main problem is to find a suitable example.

How to address the question

1 – Think about the type of situation where you may need to support a colleague.

This may be because:
- He is too busy and can't find the time to study.
- He is struggling because he lacks knowledge or experience.
- He is getting stressed for one reason or another.
- He has problems with another colleague (for example personality clash).
- He is working under the influence of alcohol.

The last two could cause you potential problems because, although on paper it may be easy to describe how you would deal hypothetically with such issues, dealing with the specifics of a situation may reveal that you did not take fully the correct approach. I would therefore recommend that you take the safest approach by sticking to simpler examples that you can exploit to your advantage.

2 – Identify the skills that you need to demonstrate.
Essentially this question is about empathy, being a good listener as well as about your ability to offer advice and help if required. All you need to do is highlight these skills throughout your answer.

QUESTION 18

What opportunities do you feel that a career in General Practice can offer you and what do you think you can offer General Practice? Please give justifications for your answers.

First Impression
Looks familiar.

How to handle the question
This is in fact two questions in one.

The first part "What opportunities do you feel that a career in General Practice can offer you" is very similar to "Why do you want to become a GP?" (See Question 11). A career in GP can offer you:
- An exposure to a variety of patients and specialties.
- An opportunity to subspecialise
- Flexible lifestyle, etc.

The second part "What do you think you can offer General Practice" is similar to "What attributes do you have that would make you a good GP?" (Question 12). What you have to offer is:
- Keenness to learn
- Empathy and ability to relate to people
- Ability to work well in teams, etc

Final Comments
This should demonstrate to you that if you prepare the key questions you should have built enough knowledge of yourself to answer any questions, as most are related.

QUESTION 19

Being a doctor can be demanding. Give an example of a stressful situation in which <u>you have</u> been involved. Outline the demands it made on <u>you personally</u> and how you coped with it. What are <u>your</u> strategies for the recognition and management of stress?

First Impression

Someone at the deanery (Oxford 2005) was keen to make you provide a personal example (the words were underlined on the form too!). Clearly this is a question that is asking you how you recognise and manage stress through an example.

Stress

1 - How you can recognise it
- Physical symptoms such as palpitations, nausea, tiredness.
- Insomnia, early morning wakening, restlessness.
- Irritability, loss of appetite, short fuse, loss of motivation.
- Substance abuse (Best not to mention it if that is how you beat stress!)
- Loss of concentration at work, becoming inefficient, lack of attention, making silly mistakes.

2 – How you can fight it
- Planning your work, prioritising and delegating.
- Asking for help from your colleagues, sharing your problems with them.
- Introducing variety into your work.
- Taking breaks, taking time off.
- Trying to anticipate difficult periods and planning accordingly.
- Learning from previous stressful experiences.
- Having time for yourself, hobbies, centres of interest outside medicine.
- Discussing problems with your friends and family.

Interview Skills Consulting

How to handle the question

1 – Identify a situation where you were stressed.
Try to choose a complex enough scenario where you were really stressed otherwise you will struggle to explain the issue convincingly and to demonstrate your full range of skills.

This may include situations where:
- You had to deal with many tasks at the same time, including several emergencies or urgent requests.

- You had to deal with a difficult or abusive patient who was taking your time, putting you behind in the rest of your work.

- You had to deal with the absence of several colleagues, including complex patients, with no senior availability.

- You were asked to do something that you did not know how to approach and were pressurised to deliver a result quickly.

2 – Develop the scenario
Once you have settled on one example, identify the skills that you used to combat your stress. For example, if you had to deal with multitasking then you will inevitably have to mention:
- How you prioritised the patients and worked with colleagues to resolve the situation.
- How you ensured that you maintained good communication
- How you ensured that your seniors knew about the issue and supported you.
- How, maybe, you negotiated with colleagues to take small breaks.

If you had to deal with a difficult patient, this will again be about team work and communication.

Go into detail about what YOU did and how it helped resolve the problem and reduce your stress level. Conclude your answer by explaining what happened when you went back home (had a bath, relaxed with family, played ping pong with friends etc) to show that you know how to relax. Finally, address the last part of the question, using some of the elements identified earlier.

85

QUESTION 20

What are the advantages and disadvantages of admitting when mistakes are made? Give examples from your own experience to illustrate your answer.

First Impression

A question about testing not only your integrity but your understanding of why integrity matters. This question is not difficult but the main problem resided in the fact that the number of words was limited to 200, which is not a lot considering everything there is to say on the subject AND the fact you had to provide examples.

When this happens you must make sure that you do not spend your entire words allowance on one section. If you have few words to write and they ask for several examples, keep your explanations to a minimum (forget the STAR system – there simply isn't enough space).

The good news is that it is an objective question i.e. it does not ask you to discuss your own feelings, but simply to quote a few facts. It makes it easier to find a good answer, but obviously also easier for everyone to have a similar answer.

Advantages of admitting when mistakes are made

- You are able to repair the mistake much more quickly because you can involve others in the process. If you kept quiet you would have to cover up or sort it all out by yourself.

- You may originally annoy people but they would be grateful for your honesty (unless you make too many mistakes). In the long term, this may encourage people to trust you more because they will know that if there is a problem you will be honest about it.

- You may save yourself a lot of trouble in the long term. If you cover up a mistake for a long time and it is then, that the patient may not forgive you. You could get sued or struck off following a complaint. If you admit the mistake and apologise early enough, the matter may be closed at an early stage.

Disadvantages of admitting when mistakes are made

- Admitting you have made a mistake could make your colleagues and patients distrust you.

- You could get sacked, sued, struck off, or all of that.

- It could lead to a loss of reputation for the whole Trust.

How to handle the question

Important note: It is very difficult to find examples where you did not admit to a mistake. Even if you ever found yourself in this position, it may not be something you would want to admit to! If you look at the question carefully, it does not actually ask for an example of both, but for examples that illustrate your answer. Most of those who got shortlisted only listed one example (on the positive side) – not withstanding the fact that it is virtually impossible to quote advantages, disadvantages and provide two examples in 200 words.

1 – Quote at least two advantages and two disadvantages. (You have to show you can think of several issues)

2 – Briefly mention one example where your admission had a positive outcome. For example:

I examined a patient in A&E and prescribed antacid, believing that the patient had indigestion. Later on he was admitted for acute anterior MI. His son was angry. I spent some time discussing the situation with him, and apologised profusely for my mistake. The son accepted my apology gratefully and thanked me for my honesty.

QUESTION 21

How have your strengths and weaknesses influenced your career choices?

First Impression

Looks easy for the "strengths" bit but the "weaknesses" part is an eternal nightmare for most candidates.

Be careful – many candidates misunderstood the question. The question is not "What are your strengths and weaknesses?" but "How did they influence your career choices?"

How to handle the question - Strengths

This question really forces you to explain how you build your career.
The trick here is to present your career as a natural evolution towards GP if possible, whilst selling the attributes that you have that would make you a good GP.

Scenario 1: All your previous jobs are fully compatible with GP, for example you have worked in Obs & Gynae for a while.

You could explain that you were equally good with your hands and at diagnosing, and that therefore you wanted to go into a discipline which combined surgery and medicine. O&G was a good option for that. At the same time you have always been good at building a good rapport with people and showing empathy. This enabled you to deal with sensitive situations, which is something that you enjoyed about O&G. However you felt that you wanted a more in-depth relationship with your patients. Also your natural curiosity and your appetite for life long learning meant that you were looking for a discipline which would help broaden your horizons and help you provide continuity of care to patients, which is why you want to become a GP.

Paediatrics

If you have done Paediatrics, you can explain that you have always been a good communicator and felt that Paediatrics would give you a good opportunity to interact with people at all levels. Being a keen learner and a curious person, you enjoyed dealing with a variety of specialties. Because you are patient you enjoyed the challenge of dealing with patients who could be potentially difficult, all this in a highly emotionally charged environment. You could then explain how you felt you wanted to deal with a broader range of the population and know that GP will give you what you are looking for: more variety not only of specialties but also age range, and long-term contact with patients.

General Medicine

If you have done a General Medicine rotation, you can easily discuss the fact that you enjoy dealing with diagnosis across a range of specialties because you have an analytical mind and enjoy communicating with patients, which attracted you to General Medicine; that you felt it also corresponded well to your personality because you had a genuine interest in people and felt you could address them as a person rather than just a surgical case. However, you also had a natural curiosity that pushed you to pursue a variety of interests that would be best explored in a GP context.

Scenario 2: You have an eclectic background with no real direction or a single track career (i.e. a lot of time spent on one specialty).
In these cases, you will have a hard time convincing anyone that you were made for GP. You have to bite the bullet and explain how you pursued your career and what motivated you until the day you actually found out properly what GP was about. Apart from that, the principles set out above apply in exactly the same way.

How to handle the question – Weaknesses

The problem is not so much to identify a weakness, but to find one that actually influenced your career choices. Typically this would be

- The fact that at medical school you were not that good with your hands and quickly realised surgery wasn't for you and therefore went into a medical specialty. You can only take this stance if you are not in a surgical

specialty. In the process make sure you reassure the reader that you are not completely useless with your hands because as a GP you may be involved in minor surgery/procedures.

- The fact that you feel uneasy working in the same environment, which prompted you to find a specialty where you could have a degree of variety (which GP provides because you can be at the surgery, in the community, doing home visits, etc)

Final Comment

Make sure you do not mistake this question for "What is your main weakness". "Being a perfectionist" or "not being able to say no to people" has never driven anybody's career.

QUESTION 22

As a GP, you will face the conflicting demands of a busy professional life, domestic pressures, patients and the NHS. Think of an occasion in the past when it was important to put someone else as your first concern over other important and conflicting priorities. This can be from any area of your life, not just paid employment. Explain the concerns, how this affected you and how you coped with it.

First Impression

It takes 2 minutes just to understand the question but at least they made an effort to avoid ambiguities.

Essentially this question is saying: Sometimes you have to prioritise something over everything else, regardless of how important these other things maybe. Give an example where you have experienced this.

How to handle the question

This question is essentially asking you to demonstrate that you are able to identify your priorities well, even when the situation is critical for you. In order to make a real impact with your answer, you will need to make sure you find a situation where you had a real dilemma, perhaps between a patient who needed to be seen and a personal issue that was really important to you. This could include situations such as:

- You are about to leave work to go back to your family. You have invited friends for dinner and were to go out to see a play. You have one complex patient and, on handing over to your replacement you find out that they are not competent enough to handle that patient. You have to stay behind and miss your dinner (patient safety first) because no one else is available.

- You are in the middle of an emergency and your wife/calls you to say that there is also an emergency at home that requires your presence.

As per previous answers you need to adopt the STAR structure. Make sure you explain the situation clearly. The key here is to highlight the dilemma that you are facing. You therefore need to explain the two emergencies and why they both required your presence.

It is easier to choose one hospital emergency and one private emergency (rather than two hospital emergencies) because you can then easily conclude that commitment to patient safety means that you have to stay at the hospital whilst trying to handle the private situation remotely until you can get away. If you do this, make sure you also explain that you had no option but to stay (i.e. you could not find anyone else to take over from you at the hospital, otherwise the recruiters might think that you are heartless and unable to delegate).

Don't forget to address the end of the question, which is asking how you were affected and how you coped with it. You can discuss how you were stressed out by not being able to go home - then refer to question 19 on how to handle stress.

Interview Skills Consulting

QUESTION 23

Patients need to trust their General Practitioners in order to share concerns and discuss sensitive issues. Think of an occasion in the past where it was important to maintain someone's trust. This could be from any area of your life, not just paid employment. Describe the situation; explain why trust was important; and what you did to maintain the trust.

First Impression

The question is straight-forward enough and the description leads you through a possible answer. It only remains to find a suitable example.

Suitable example

1 - Work based

This would include situations where:

- A patient told you to maintain confidentiality and you had to reassure them that you would do so.

- A patient may not be compliant unless they feel they can trust you.

- A patient is sceptical because he/she has had bad experiences with doctors in the past.

2 – Non-work based

This would include situations where:

- A friend or relative has a problem they do not wish you to divulge to others.

- A friend needs support with a personal issue.

93

QUESTION 24

Describe the methods by which you keep yourself up to date and interested in medicine, and how you identify your own learning needs.

First Impression
A standard question, which you should have no problem answering provided you come away from the generalities and provide a degree of detail.

Methods you can use to keep up to date.
- Attending courses (name a couple you attended in the past year or so)

- Reading journals (name those you read: BMJ, Lancet, specialty papers) and the frequency at which you read them.

- Reading up on the internet: Cochrane, Medline, other websites (name them, it sounds more credible).

- Attending training sessions at the hospital (how frequently?). Attending and participating in journal clubs, case review meetings.

- Teaching others (you can learn by doing teaching as you have to prepare!)

How you can identify your learning needs
- Throughout your work by picking up on problems that you encounter during the day.

- By observing and discussing with colleagues.

- By getting feedback from colleagues and patients.

- By comparing your skills with what is expected of you (training schedule, appraisal records, etc)

QUESTION 25

Describe a time when you had to deal with a sceptical patient. How did you address the situation? What was the outcome?

First Impression

This question is all about communication. All you need to do is find the best example and use the STAR technique.

How to handle the question

1 – Identify why a patient may be sceptical

- They do not trust you for one reason or another. Maybe they have prior bad experiences with friends or relatives that would make them doubt your word.

- They may have information from the media (for example through TV, newspapers or the internet) that gives them a different perspective.

- They may be medically aware i.e. they are scientists or linked to the medical profession. They require more information than your average patient.

- They may have personal beliefs (against conventional treatment for example) or simply a language problem.

- They have a problem with you (e.g. a male patient being suspicious of a female doctor, a patient trusting older doctors only, etc).

- Your proposed options may be counter-intuitive.

2 – Identify what this question is about.

Essentially there are two factors to consider:

(i) As a doctor you should do your best to ensure that the patient is fully informed. You cannot force the patient to do anything, but you need to demonstrate that you have done everything in your power to act in the best interest of that patient. This means that:

- You should explore the concerns that the patient has and address any underlying issues. For example, if they distrust conventional medicine, you should investigate the reasons behind this concern.

- You should make sure that the patient receives all the information that you can give them. This could be through the involvement of other professionals (for example by involving another colleague, a nurse or referring to a suitable specialist) or by giving a leaflet.

- You should ensure that you address the patient in a way they can understand (basic English if needed, interpreter, diagrams) and that they have time to digest the information and ask questions to you or others.

- If you are getting stuck with the patient, then you always have the option of asking a senior colleague how you should handle the situation (remember – you should be aware of your limitations!)

(ii) The patient has the right to make a decision for themselves. So if your particular patient still disagreed with you at the end, don't panic but make it clear that you documented their disagreement. It is their right to disagree and your duty to accept that they can do so.

Final comments

Once you have found the right example, describing the situation is fairly straight forward using the STAR technique. Do make sure that you address the full question by mentioning what happened at the end.

QUESTION 26

Describe a time when you have been involved in a cost-saving exercise in the workplace. What are the issues associated with cost saving?

First Impression

This is a most unusual question, particularly as it seems to be fairly discriminatory against those who have little managerial experience as they will inevitably struggle to find interesting examples. The question also restricts the range of examples that you can use by imposing an example in the work environment.

How to approach the question

Think about what could constitute cost-saving. It does not have to be a situation where you are in charge of a big budget or where you are organising big projects. During your day-to-day activities you are constantly confronted with choices you have to make, some of which are more onerous than others. Examples could include:

- Identifying a procedure which takes a long time to perform or uses too many resources. By pointing this out and discussing the situation with colleagues, you may start a review process (audit) which ultimately leads to a more efficient practice and hence lower costs for your trusts.

- Identifying that you are often prescribing a particular drug which a more expensive than another one. You subsequently took steps to ensure that you and your team took note of this when prescribing.

- Ensuring that the discharge process for patients is as efficient as it can be so that you can see more patients and therefore cut the cost of dealing with each patient. You may have done that by becoming more efficient in your own work, encouraging your own team to work more efficiently and ensuring that members of the multidisciplinary team work more efficiently together towards cutting discharge times.

- Implementing a change in the way outpatients are booked in order to minimise "Do Not Attend" patients or to introducing a system designed to minimise the number of overrunning clinics.

Once you have found a suitable example, follow the STAR structure. In this case, it means:

- Identifying what the issue was and why cost saving was needed (e.g. where did the inefficiencies lie)

- Explaining the action that you took which could range from a discussion with colleagues all the way to a full audit.

- Explaining what happened as a result of your actions. If you can, try to be specific by quantifying the impact (e.g. the number of patients seen increased by 10%, the number of DNAs reduced by 20%, etc). It gives it more credibility.

Final Comments

Try to bring several skills into play. This is a good opportunity to talk about:
- organisational skills (becoming efficient through better time management)
- team playing (involving others and seeking their opinion and help)
- communication and negotiation skills (convincing others)

The question may also require you to discuss the issues associated with cost saving. If this is the case, you may wish to address the following points:

- Cost saving can affect staff, clients and quality positively or negatively depending on the nature and the extent of the saving.

- Cost saving can bring efficiency but it can also mean losing quality.

- Cost saving in the NHS is a sensitive issue for the general population. All tax payers want to pay less tax but cost savings also often attract negative news headlines. It is a Catch 22 situation.

- Cost saving can affect staff morale.

QUESTION 27

Describe a time when you made an assumption and subsequently changed your mind.

First Impression

A vague question but with a great potential to help you shine above the others if you find the right example. Again, it is very much a matter of spending a few minutes identifying a suitable situation before launching into writing it up.

How to handle the question

1 – Identify the type of situation where you may have made assumptions.
It could be a situation where

- A colleague mentioned something to you which you assumed was correct when it wasn't. As a result you did not take appropriate action.

- You assumed that a patient had previously been informed of a diagnosis but had not; or you assumed that a patient had understood the information that you had given them when in fact they had not.

- A patient came accompanied by someone to A&E. You assumed that they were related when in fact it was just a friend or a taxi driver.

- You wanted to admit someone and assumed that there would be no issues. In fact it turned out that they had dependants at home or a dog to look after.

- A patient had a rash and you assumed they wanted to be treated when in fact it did not bother them at all.

- You assumed that a patient was competent when, after further investigation, he/she turns out to be demented and could not retain information.

- You assumed that an elderly patient wanted to stay in their current house because they had an emotional attachment but in fact they wanted to go into a home. Or conversely, you assumed that the patient wanted to go into a nursing home when in fact they wanted to stay at home.

2 – Explain your actions clearly and in detail

You must provide the detail of:

- How you came to realise that you had made the wrong assumption i.e. what prompted you to think that you had got it wrong. Did the patient or a colleague say something? Did tests reveal more information? Did you read up on the subject?

- How you reacted once you had identified you had made the wrong assumption. Here, you will need to show your initiative and speed at resolving what could have become a big problem. This may involve apologising to the relevant people (patient, senior, etc), informing your seniors if necessary and then taking any appropriate action to resolve the problem.

- How the incident ended and what you learnt from the experience.

Final Comment

There are many skills that can be introduced in this answer:

- Integrity (by admitting that you made a mistake and apologising)
- Team work (by ensuring that seniors are aware of the incident if they need to be informed)
- Communication (by making sure you liaise with the right people at the right level – particularly if correcting your mistake requires a lot of additional communication)

ISCMEDICAL
Interview Skills Consulting

QUESTION 28

Describe a time when you felt unable to be open and honest with a patient. Why did you find it difficult and what did you do about it? What was the outcome?

First Impression

Not an easy question unless you have some experience of dealing with delicate situations. You will also need to make sure that your answer does not present you as someone who is hiding information from patients just for the sake of having an easy life at work.

How to handle the question

1 – Identify possible situations & why you found it difficult
This could a situation where:

- You had to break bad news to a patient who was vulnerable (a frail and elderly patient, someone who was distressed). You found it difficult either because you did not want to distress the patient further or because you felt that the distress caused would outweigh the benefit of being open.

- A mistake had been made, the patient was behaving aggressively or was insisting on an explanation and you did want to discuss anything before you had the chance to talk to other members of your team.

- Your patient was the partner or relative of another patient. Being honest and open may mean breaching confidentiality.

- You needed to report the patient to a relevant authority (DVLA, social services, police, etc) but could not face telling the patient in case he/she reacted badly.

2 – Explain in detail how you handled it

Handling such situation can be done using a wide range of skills and personal qualities, which you will be required to demonstrate through your answer. This could involve:

- Asking for help from a senior colleague to discuss how you should be handling the situation and how you should approach the patient (note: this is always a safe option whenever you are having problems addressing an issue).

- Discussing the issue with a friend and rationalising the problem in your mind. Sometimes, taking some time thinking things through can help make the right decision. It can also help you deal with any feelings of discomfort that you may be facing.

- Getting someone to sit with you through the consultation that you have with the patient so that you have the strength to go through with it. It can also benefit the patient to have an extra person in the room.

- Spending more time talking to the patient to build a greater rapport, gain a greater understanding of who they are and how they might react so that you can address the issue at the right level eventually.

Final comments

In this question, there is actually very little else you can do to resolve the matter other than somehow finding the strength to do the right thing. In most cases this will involve talking to someone or finding the courage by yourself. You may therefore find it difficult at first to draw 250 words out of this situation.

An important part of the answer is about the feelings that you experienced and the explanation of the dilemma that you were facing at the time. You should therefore ensure that you give it appropriate space in your answer.

Also, make sure that you do not simply say that you sought help from a friend or colleague but give some explanation of how your discussion helped resolve the problem.